REACHING THE GIFTED

A Resource Book
for Affective Development

Barbara Dixon
John Meyer
Allan Hardy

With Forewords by
Sidney J. Parnes
and
Sandra M. Shiner

Curriculum Series / 51

OISE Press

The Ontario Institute for Studies in Education

The Ontario Institute for Studies in Education has three prime functions: to conduct programs of graduate study in education, to undertake research in education, and to assist in the implementation of the findings of educational studies. The Institute is a college chartered by an Act of the Ontario Legislature in 1965. It is affiliated with the University of Toronto for graduate studies purposes.

The publications program of the Institute has been established to make available information and materials arising from studies in education, to foster the spirit of critical inquiry, and to provide a forum for the exchange of ideas about education. The opinions expressed should be viewed as those of the contributors.

© The Ontario Institute for Studies in Education 1986
    252 Bloor Street West
    Toronto, Ontario
    M5S 1V6

Canadian Cataloguing in Publication Data

Dixon, Barb, 1947-
    Reaching the gifted

(Curriculum series ; 51)
Includes bibliographies.
ISBN 0-7744-0299-7

1. Gifted children — Education (Elementary).
2. Self-perception — Study and teaching (Elementary).
I. Meyer, John R., 1934-   . II. Hardy, Allan.
III. Title. IV. Series: Curriculum series (Ontario
Institute for Studies in Education) ; 51.

LC3993.22.D59 1986   371.95'3   C86-094072-1

ISBN 0-7744-0299-7   Printed in Canada
    2   3   4   5   UTP   09   98   88   78

Contents

Forewords

I have known Barbara Dixon, the senior author of this book, for a number of years, first meeting her at one of our annual meetings of The Creative Problem Solving Institute in Buffalo. Next, I participated in several programs she directed in Canada. Finally, I became most knowledgeable of her visionary qualities when she proposed an experimental program for her gifted students at Epcot, as one of our Creative Education Foundation's future creative problem-solving workshops at Epcot Centre. She organized this group and served as a facilitator in the pilot program — a first for school-age students, in general, and for gifted students, in particular. The program was highly successful and will be followed next year with two adaptations for specific groups in her country. I appreciated first-hand how effectively Barbara thinks and works with her students. So I am most pleased to see her ideas emerging now in book form, co-authored by John Meyer and Allan Hardy.

The authors have assembled here a variety of interesting, engaging exercises and materials that appear to be highly suitable for nurturing creative ability as well as for subject matter purposes and psychosocial or affective objectives.

Although I have never had the opportunity to work regularly with gifted students in the classroom setting, I would be fascinated to do so using the materials the authors offer. Moreover, I would expect the same would be true for a teacher of any student, assuming that teacher cared about the affective objectives the authors outline and the thinking skills promoted by these kinds of educational experiences.

I hope this book will encourage more and more teachers everywhere to embark on more engaging, creative patterns of teaching and challenging their students. This is essential for teachers of the gifted, who may well "tune out" or drop out without such challenge to their talents. But typical or average students as well ought to be highly motivated by teachers who use approaches like the ones suggested in this book.

Sidney J. Parnes, Chairman,
Board of Creative Education Foundation, Buffalo,
and Visiting Professor of Creative Studies,
Buffalo State University College

"God gave us a gifted child, but he forgot to include a set of instructions." So begins the frustrating story of gifted five-year-old Jimmy, and the struggle that his parents experienced in trying to find an educational setting which would allow their child to blossom and make use of his prodigious intellectual and scientific gifts without harassment and ridicule from the formal school system and his social peers. This story illustrates the need for a volume such as *Reaching the Gifted*.

As the authors have rightly stated, most of the literature on the gifted focusses on their intellectual potential. Very little of the literature examines the psychosocial needs of these individuals. The reason for this is not clear. Perhaps it is due to the fact that formal school systems in general have not seen it as their prime mandate to cater to the personal side of knowledge. Teaching the three R's and "the basics" related to cognitive development is a more comfortable domain for most teachers. The affective side of human development is an area which few educational systems tackle with enthusiasm for any group of learners. To suggest, as this book does, that the gifted have specific psychosocial needs which must be identified and facilitated is an even less familiar concept. The present volume therefore tackles two major, but generally overlooked, issues in education: affective education in general and the affective neeeds of the gifted in particular.

The authors give a sensitive and useful description of the specific psychosocial needs of gifted students. The ensuing chapters focus on practical curriculum adaptations of the self in the lives of others (human rights, seniors) and help the gifted understand themselves more fully through useful exercises in the areas of visualization and various types of bibliotherapy. The materials are clearly written and have the potential to be either teacher-directed or student-directed. This is a useful alternative in differentiated curriculum materials for the gifted. Older students could also be encouraged to adapt exercises and questions to their own interests.

At the same time that general enthusiastic support is given to the approach of this volume, a note of caution must be sounded. As has already been stated, very few teachers have been able to take sufficient training to be experts about the needs of the gifted. Erroneous assumptions therefore abound regarding the behaviors and reactions of these students (for example, "since the gifted have already been blessed with more abilities than most, they shouldn't need extra or different attention"). Further, through the courses I offer on affective education, I have found that very few teachers are initially comfortable with the different learning environments and techniques which are necessary to "teach" affective types of education successfully.

Teachers must learn to feel confident about their own creativity, risk-taking, and self-knowledge before they can facilitate this growth in their students. Specific training workshops should be offered to help teachers successfully implement the exercises in this handbook. Otherwise, an important journey to the soul may remain a purely intellectual pursuit.

Sandra M. Shiner
Department of Special Education
Ontario Institute for Studies in Education, Toronto

Preface

The mind is not a vessel to be filled, it is a fire to be kindled.
Plutarch

If one were to speculate upon the primary objective of gifted education, these noble words of Plutarch would be the perfect place to begin. In recent years many publications regarding the education of the exceptional student have articulated this sentiment and also created a public awareness of the intellectual needs of the gifted child. However, very little of this literature has covered the affective domain, an area so important in the social development of the gifted learner. To rectify this discrepancy, the authors of *Reaching the Gifted* have included within these pages numerous strategies and techniques which will enhance the personal, emotional, and social growth of the gifted student.

The structure of *Reaching the Gifted* is based on these same growth dimensions. We believe that if an individual possesses a sense of self, then it is possible to share these positive attributes within society. The chapters on societal rights and senior/youth interaction exemplify the level of moral development possible for the gifted.

A unique feature of this book is that the many exercises outlined within have been field-tested with children, aged 8 to 14. Samples of these encounters are included. Other exercises, however, particularly in the chapter on visualization, are left open-ended so as not to inhibit the creative process.

In the world of spiritual symbolism, fire is equated with strength. Scientifically, fire is perhaps the ultimate chemical transformation. The authors hope that this book will allow both educators and parents to spark, strengthen, and transform our greatest resource — the human mind.

Acknowledgments

The authors wish to thank the following for their assistance in the production of this book:

David Baldwin, Director of Education, Dufferin County Board of Education; Hazel Bowen, Consultant for Gifted and Guidance, Ottawa Board of Education; William Dixon, Landmark College, Vermont, for permissions assistance; Karen Epps, word processor operator; Ann Geh, for her story "Withdrawn" in chapter 7; Lillian Lahe, Resource teacher for the Gifted, York Region; Martha Light, Education Officer, Ministry of Education, Toronto; Mary Sue McCarthy, Professor, Faculty of Education, York University; Leonard Popp, Associate Professor, Brock University; Stanley Robinson, formerly Director of Education, Dufferin County Board of Education; Ken Trumpour, Superintendent, Dufferin Board of Education.

Lastly, the authors extend a special thanks to Sam Dixon for his illustrations in the book and cover art.

Introduction: Bridging Theory and Practice

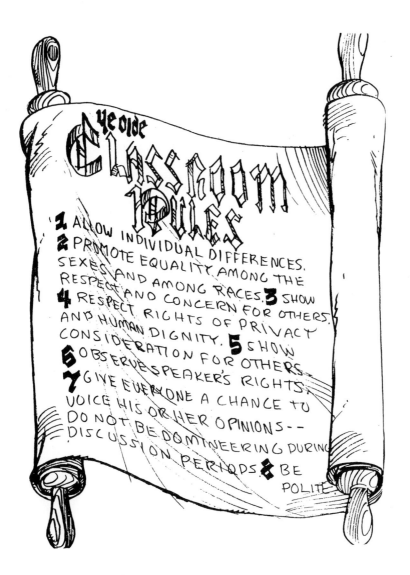

Ye olde Classroom Rules

1 ALLOW INDIVIDUAL DIFFERENCES.
2 PROMOTE EQUALITY AMONG THE SEXES AND AMONG RACES. 3 SHOW RESPECT AND CONCERN FOR OTHERS. 4 RESPECT RIGHTS OF PRIVACY AND HUMAN DIGNITY. 5 SHOW CONSIDERATION FOR OTHERS. 6 OBSERVE SPEAKER'S RIGHTS. 7 GIVE EVERYONE A CHANCE TO VOICE HIS OR HER OPINIONS -- DO NOT BE DOMINEERING DURING DISCUSSION PERIODS 8 BE POLITE.

> "Professor's" what they call me
> I'm known throughout the school
> As some straight-laced goody-goody
> Who never breaks a rule.
> If I get in trouble
> It makes the new headlines —
> I guess it's a conspiracy
> To be among good minds.
> I wish they knew the real me.
> The one that stays inside,
> The one known to my "gifted" friends
> But to others, stays inside.

(Girl, age 13, Delisle, 1984)

The literature on the gifted child abounds with information for promoting the "intellectual" aspects of teaching and learning for the gifted student. Yet, only some one percent of this same literature focusses on the psychosocial aspects of such teaching and learning. Only recently has significant attention been given to these "affective" dimensions of total growth.

Among the reasons for this lack of attention to the psychosocial aspects of educating the gifted are radical shifts in familial and social structures; the assumption on the part of parents and teachers that the gifted student can adjust to those structures more easily than students with other exceptionalities; the belief that teachers' responsibilities should be restricted to the "intellectual" aspects; and, perhaps, the teacher's personal sense of inadequacy caused by a lack of preparation in gifted education or the constraints of a system.

When the gifted thirteen-year-old says: "I wish they knew the real me. The one that stays inside, the one known to my 'gifted' friends, but to others, stays inside" (Delisle, 1984), or the twelve-year-old who says, while at a summer camp for the gifted child, "I think that people who aren't smart probably have more friends. People who aren't so smart are nicer than smart people," we become conscious that psychosocial needs are very much a part of being gifted.

In addition to this personal need, there are the usual expectations of others. Very often, the parents of the gifted, as well as a considerable proportion of society, expect that the gifted child will "pay back" or "return" something to society as if parents or society were responsible for this exceptionality. "We want each child to give something back to the world," said the parents of four gifted daughters. However noble and altruistic the conviction, there are often debilitating effects from undue pressures and from forming a self-concept based upon the expectations of others. The total growth of the child is closely interrelated to the psychosocial dimensions of growth and learning. As Passow says, "The pursuit of excellence along many dimensions is determined by the affective climate" (1985).

Another factor that confuses the issue is the variety of definitions of the gifted learner and the absence within those of attention to the psychosocial dimensions. Two definitions by Drews and Tannenbaum that span a decade come closest to expressing the totality of the gifted learner. Drews states:

> "The gifted, in my view, can be simply defined as those who show themselves, in relation both to their age group and to all others, as more fully human." (1975, p. 1)

And Tannenbaum writes:

> "Giftedness denotes their potential for becoming critically acclaimed performers or exemplary producers of ideas in spheres of activity that enhance the moral, physical, emotional, social, intellectual, or aesthetic life of humanity." (1983, p. 86)

Though there is no inclusion of the affective nature of education for the gifted in the definition in *Programming for the Gifted* of the Ontario Ministry of Education (1985, p. 6), there is the noticeable recognition of this component in the total conceptual framework and in one chapter, perhaps intentionally placed before the chapter on cognitive development. This recognition of "advanced affective capacity", requiring the needs of social acceptance, integration within self and among others, opportunities for leadership, positive self-concept, a personal values system, and self-actualization (pp. 20-21), is a significant contribution to the resources available for systems planning and implementation.

There are no compelling research findings that definitively state that the gifted are any less developed or prone to psychosocial problems than those with other exceptionalities or those without exceptionalities. There is research that suggests that particular psychosocial needs, traits, and responses of the gifted and talented must be attended to in order to avoid or remediate problems. These human and personal needs are placed within the context of a changing society whose members tend to experience:
- a crisis in personal and societal values;
- conflicts in value priorities;
- an increased ability to cope with radically different family structures — single parents, latch-key situations, and general instability.

A Conceptual Framework or Model

Curriculum or program designers have an array of models to draw upon for providing a basis for a structure. Some use Maslow's hierarchy of needs or Krathwohl's affective domain (see sec. 3, *Programming*, 1985). Our preference is for a model (Morse et al., 1980) based on three comprehensive psychosocial need dimensions:

(a) *Self-Adequacy:*   the personal dimension of self-concept (who one is) combined with self-esteem (how one feels about self).

(b) *Social Competency:*   abilities to communicate and inter-relate with others.

(c) *Emotional Engagement:*   motivation expressed in personal satisfaction and appreciation.

These three dimensions are interrelated and not hierarchical. In other words, if there is appropriate growth in self-adequacy, this may lead to emotional engagement, which might promote the acquisition of social competencies. Or the direction might start with the realization of social competencies which lead to an enhanced sense of self-adequacy, which then provides a basis for emotional engagements. (See Figure 1.)

We can take this a step further by placing it within the context of acceptable phases of learning through various instructional activities. The content of any of the following chapters might engage the learner by focussing on any one or all successive phases of learning, namely:

Awareness: (attention to what is initially happening)

Sensitivity: (interaction with the environment: animate, inanimate)

Reflection and Valuing: (interpretations and judgments)

Application/Action: (positive results, acts, closure)

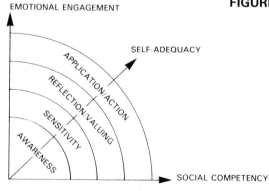

FIGURE 1

If we apply this scenario to the literature or language arts activities in this book, we could demonstrate that the teacher and student(s) attend to (a) what is happening and/or the problems in the story; (b) the interpersonal relationships or the reaction to the environment; (c) what is implied by the characters and the events in terms of consequences, alternatives; and (d) what actions are appropriate, what are the results?

The teacher — sometimes with the students — will reflect on the implications for growth in self-adequacy and/or social competencies, and whether or not the student does get emotionally engaged or might do so in subsequent personal behaviors of a similar context.

Hopefully, these learning activities do respond to the need for understanding self and others; for development of communication skills, conflict resolution, negotiating; and for coping with emotions as many educators of the gifted have suggested (Whitmore, 1983).

Psychosocial Deficits and the Gifted

It has been said that "the gifted must be seen as average with gifts, not as superior with faults" (Manaster & Powell, 1983, p. 73). It is also recognized that the gifted are in many ways similar and vulnerable to the same forces affecting the typical student. But this same vulnerability may be increased, leading to psychosocial jeopardy. To use the model of Manaster and Powell, gifted students may be "*out of state, phase, and or sync*", any one of these:

Condition	Description	Psychosocial Location
Out of Stage	Gifted adolescents are different from *average* adolescents in their stage of cognitive and related development and/or in the quality and variety of their talents.	Cognitive developmental and talents
Out of Phase	Gifted adolescents, possibly because they are *out of stage*, have abilities and interests at variance from their *average* peers and are themselves unable or unwilling to fit in socially due to these apparent differences.	Social
Out of Sync.	Gifted adolescents, either because they are *out of stage* or *out of phase* or both, *feel* that they are different whether in positive or negative, self-enhancing or self-deflating ways, and feel they do not, should not or cannot fit in.	Psychological

Source: G. J. Manaster and P. M. Powell, "A Framework for Understanding Gifted Adolescents' Psychological Maladjustment," *Roeper Review*, 6:2 (November 1983), pp. 70-73. Reprinted by permission of the authors.

These are conditions that educators need to be aware of and to work with as directly and sensitively as possible. Experts in gifted education have provided much commentary on the subject (Whitmore, 1980; Altman, 1983; Roedell, 1984). Years ago, Leta Hollingworth, one of the pioneers in gifted education, set a precedent in her now famous statement that "it is difficult to have the intelligence of an adult and the emotions of a child in a childish body." (1942, p. 282)

The lists of psychosocial characteristics are numerous. They are very often combined with various cognitive items because there are distinctions but not necessarily clear separations. The works of Altman (1983) and Webb et al. (1982) are particularly useful here. As a synthesis of these characteristics, I offer the following six categories:

- *Introspective* — Self-analysis may be extreme: usually estimate of strengths and weaknesses: tends to criticism of self/others: some identity confusion: ability to define own and others goals.

- *Sensitive to Feelings and Expectations of Self and Others* — Degrees of copability to life in spite of adverse societal reactions; may develop despondency over sense of powerlessness, inadequacy, impatience, intolerance, or alienation; unusual emotional depth and empathy.

- *Responsive to Personal and Social Values* — Earlier sense of altruism: accentuated fears of death, war, violence, injustice, dangerous world; strong need for consistency between values and personal actions; understand values underlying social issues of interest to them; ability to explain reasons for choice/action; capacity for extended morality, social responsibility, realistic dilemmas.

- *Idealistic, Perfectionist* — Reluctant to accept authoritarian pronouncements without critical examination; tendency to organize people, things, situations in order to solve problems; high expectations of self and others may cause difficult relationships, and/or procrastination.

- *Non-Conformist, Humorist* — Tends to associate with older children or adults; independence; values, ideas of peers; keen sense of displaying and appreciating humor; manipulative skills to retaliate or gain control; many rules, norms, seem illogical.

- *Imaginative, Energetic, Enthusiastic* — High levels; long attention spans; goal directed; may read excess meaning into ordinary situations; needs help in interpreting meanings; more divergent thinker stressing differences, alternatives.

Remediation

For the sake of simplicity, suggestions for remedial methods both in the home and in the school setting are divided into two broad categories: *PERSONAL* psychological and *SOCIAL* psychological. One might describe these as "minimal conditions" for remediation. Depending upon the situation, it is desirable to expand those conditions to the maximum limits.

(a) *PERSONAL:* convey sense of success, opportunity to develop self-direction and self-control; setting limits, realistic expectations; guidance in learning to cope with perfectionism and supersensitivity; balance of cooperation and competition; good role models, student-centred classroom; promotion of interest, curiosity, assertiveness; affiliation and self-esteem needs to be satisfied; provide opportunities for choices; stress management by positive self-talk, calming, humor, diversions; anticipatory praise; expression of feelings.

(b) *SOCIAL* : promote communication of feelings, trust, sense of acceptance, climate of affirmation of worth; constructive feedback from teacher and peers; need for variety of peer groups; intentional development of social skills and leadership potential, particularly the following SOCIAL SKILLS:

   (1) increased awareness and understanding of the social world, the needs and feelings of others, the relationship between emotions and behavior, the nature of groups and group dynamics;

   (2) developed social skills related to communicating, cooperating, building affiliations and mutually supportive relationships, functioning in a group, and handling conflict;

   (3) developed personal–emotional skills for coping with stress related to personal needs and controlling self to attain desired social consequences;

   (4) increased ability to use constructive social feedback to modify behavior and direct personal growth.

Perrone (1982) and colleagues have developed a valuable identification measure with two clusters of items directly related to:

   (a) *Social Awareness:* the gifted student has a repertoire of behaviors including: the identification of certain social and interpersonal issues as important; the organization of activities to solve the problem; adaptability to meet changing conditions; understanding the values underlying social issues; and the facility to explain the reasons for making a given choice.

   (b) *Social Effectiveness:* relates well with older children and adults, responds more quickly and appropriately than peers, likes to share experiences with peers, displays a sense of humor, and demonstrates independent action.

These behaviors are facilitated in the desirable classroom activities, for example:

• class meetings for social problem-solving with open-ended dialogue;
• role-playing, sociodrama, and pantomime;

- use of content of language arts, science, and social sciences;
- options, choices, and free activity times;
- individualized activities such as research tasks;
- much opportunity for problem-solving and divergent thinking; calming techniques; stress reduction.

The "curriculum" as viewed as a particular conglomerate of sequenced learning activities, specific objectives, and evaluative procedures can and should be productive in the total growth of the gifted/talented learner. Attention must be paid to those components of sequence, specificity, and evaluation. The field of gifted education has matured sufficiently to provide a wide variety of excellently designed curricula "that build on and challenge children's strengths while allowing for guided development in areas of weakness." (Roedell et al., 1980)

Evaluation

There are few specific references to evaluation procedures in the chapters that follow. Evaluation is very much a personalized and programmatic issue. The essential questions of evaluation: of whom? by whom? for what purposes? must be appropriately answered. A number of fine measures are now available for evaluating psychosocial components. For example, three areas that might be examined are:

1. *Behavior change:* systematic observations, anecdotal records; self-reports;
2. *Improved self-perception:* self-concept inventories;
3. *Improved social skills and attitudes:* sociometrics, observations, anecdotal reports, attitudinal inventories.

Much of what happens in classrooms is directly related to the leadership and competencies of the teacher. For this reason, it is important to indicate, at the very least, the ideal qualities of a teacher for the gifted/talented.

Desirable Teacher Characteristics

The teacher as "facilitator" of the learning process is certainly a very powerful agent in the total growth endeavor. One eleven-year-old gifted boy expressed it this way (Delisle, p. 55):

"Teachers encourage originality and creativity, stimulate your imagination, and care about you personally as well as schoolwise. They understand you're not perfect. They are friendly, they smile and make you feel good and happy. Teachers can help."

Our conceptual framework of growth development is equally applicable to the teacher of the gifted. The teacher must be strong in personal adequacy, emotional strength, and social competency. These are prerequisites for an atmosphere in which cognitive risk-taking and empathic skills development can freely occur.

In addition to this maturity and the generic competencies of any effective teacher, that is, enthusiasm, personal interest in students, sincerity and honesty, good listener, likeable, concerned, there are specific characteristics summarized by Barbara Clark (pp. 366-68) and adapted here; characteristics that promote the growth of:

The Inquiring Mind

1. Involve the pupil in incomplete situations.
2. Lead the pupil to a question or problem that puzzles.
3. Ask the kind of question that is not readily answerable by a study of the "lesson."
4. Permit the pupil to suggest additional or alternative answers.
5. Encourage the pupil to guess or hypothesize about the unknown or untested.
6. Entertain even wild or far-out suggestions by pupils.
7. Ask the pupil to support answers or opinions by providing evidence.
8. Provide material and time for the pupil to develop ideas.
9. Ask "How would you predict?" questions.
10. Make "If, then" statements.

Self-Respect

1. Move freely among the pupils.
2. Engage in positive redirection, attend pupils closely, give individual attention.
3. Praise, smile, laugh, nod, show authentic feelings.
4. Admit errors openly.
5. Listen to each pupil's opinion.
6. Use groups discussion to allow feelings to be expressed, to solve problems.
7. Have the pupil write stories about self.
8. Take time for activities in developing self-esteem.
9. Tell the pupils about their work.
10. Plan and evaluate cooperatively.

Respect for Others

1. Ask pupils to help others.
2. Help pupils to solve problems of disturbing others.
3. Ask the class to discuss differences in people.
4. Discuss controversial issues with the class.
5. Ask the class about how they think others might feel.
6. Use value clarification techniques.
7. Encourage social interchange and cooperation.

Sense of Competence

Aiding self-esteem:
1. Have pupils find their own information.
2. Provide the time and opportunity for pupils to use special aids, language aids, tape recorders, learning centres, and so on.
3. Tell the pupils when they have done a good job.
4. Allow pupils space to display their own work.
5. Give alternative ways of working when a pupil shows a lack of interest or frustration.
6. Keep a record of work accomplished (visibly and cooperatively).
7. Give fewer directions, less criticisms, less lecturing; encourage participation.

Sense of Responsibility for One's Own Conduct

1. Have pupils make their own analysis of subject matter.
2. Have pupils find detailed facts and information on their own.
3. Have pupils work independently on what concerns them.
4. Encourage self-discipline on the part of the pupil.
5. Withhold judgment on pupil's behavior or work.
6. Encourage the pupil to put his or her ideas to a test.
7. Evaluate the work of different pupils by different standards, cooperatively.
8. Use self-evaluation.

Sense of Commitment

1. By showing concern for peers and others.
2. Advising, suggesting, or interpreting.
3. Comforting or reassuring.
4. Fixing something.
5. Protecting, warning, defending.
6. Getting help for somebody else, helping another accomplish a task, or helping out in distress.
7. Offering needed help.

Source: Adapted from Barbara Clark, *Growing Up Gifted* (Toronto: Charles Merill, 1983), pp. 366-68. By permission of the publishers.

Just as it is expected that teachers of the gifted/talented will provide options and flexibility for their students, so the learning materials for classroom activities in this book provide a challenge to these teachers to be flexible in their application. They have been field-tested in classrooms with students between the ages of 8 and 14. The emphasis of the materials has been on the three growth dimensions of personal, emotional, and social relevance as outlined above.

Whether the teacher is in an enrichment or self-contained or another alternative structure, she or he can adapt the materials. But whatever the program context, the teacher should be sensitive to the issue of reinforcement of concepts, skills, and attitudes in order to promote desired growth. The extension of activities by modification, creativity, and supplement is a natural consequence of a challenging environment. It is undesirable to use these materials as "fillers" or to consider them as "teacher-proofed" recipes.

The topics selected for each chapter are primarily self-contained; they were chosen because they are considered to be developmentally interesting and appropriate. They are topics that have aroused interest in classrooms and that directly relate to psychosocial development. A brief introduction to each chapter attempts to review the relevant theory and resources followed by the classroom activities.

There are no guarantees that the use of these materials will assure either emotional growth or balance among gifted children. But consistent application and expansion of these activities will at least provide a challenge and opportunity for the type of psychosocial development desperately needed and deserved.

As Silverman says:

> "If ever there was a good reason for gifted programmes, it would be to provide a safe psychological environment for the emotional development of these children. If we fail to provide the kind of understanding which they so desperately need, we transform emotional sensitivity into emotional disturbance, and we risk losing these individuals permanently. This is a risk none of us can afford to take." (1983)

Suggested Readings

Altman, R. "Social-Emotional Development of Gifted Children and Adolescents: A Research Model." *Roeper Review*, 6:2 (November, 1983), pp. 65-68.

Bloom, B. *Developing Talent in Young People.* New York: Ballantine Books, 1985.

Clark, B. *Growing Up Gifted: Developing the Potential of Children at Home and at School.* 2nd edition. Toronto: Charles Merrill Pub. Co., 1983.

Delisle, J. R. *Gifted Children Speak Out.* New York: Walker & Co., 1984.

Drews, Elizabeth M. "The Gifted Student: A Researcher's View." In *Gifted and Talented: Developing Elementary and Secondary School Programmes,* edited by Bruce O. Boston (Council for Exceptional Children, 1975). ED 117886, Reston, Virginia.

Gallagher, James J. *Teaching The Gifted Child.* 3rd edition. Boston: Allyn & Bacon, Inc., 1985.

Gowan, John Curtis; Khatena, Joe; and Torrance, E. Paul, eds. *Educating the Ablest*, a book of readings. 2nd edition. Itasca, Ill.: F. E. Peacock Publishers, Inc., 1979.

Hollingworth, L. S. *Children Above 180 I.Q., Standford-Binet.* Yonkers-on-Hudson, N.Y.: World Book, 1942.

Maker, C. June. *Curriculum Development for the Gifted.* Rookville, Maryland: Aspen Systems Corporation, 1982.

Manaster, G. J., and Powell, P. M. "A Framework for Understanding Gifted Adolescents' Psychological Maladjustment." *Roeper Review*, 6:2 (November 1983), pp. 70-73.

Morse, William C.; Ardizzone, J.; Macdonald, C.; and Pasick, P. *Affective Education for Special Children and Youth* (Council for Exceptional Children & ERIC, 1980), Reston, Virginia.

Passow, A. H. "Intellectual Development of the Gifted". In *Essays on the Intellect*, edited by F. R. Link. Alexandria, VA: Association for Supervision & Curriculum Development, 1985.

Perrone, P. A. "Issues in Social and Emotional Development: Giftedness: A Personal-Social Phenomenon." *Roeper Review*, 6:2 (November 1983), pp. 63-65.

Programming for the Gifted: A Support Document. Toronto: Ontario Ministry of Education, 1986.

Roedell, W. C. "Vulnerabilities of Highly Gifted Children." *Roeper Review*, 6:3 (February 1984), pp. 127-30.

Roedell, W. C.; Jackson, N. E.; and Robinson, H. B. *Gifted Young Children.* New York: Teachers' College Press, Columbia University, 1980.

Silverman, L. K. "Issues in Affective Development for the Gifted." In *A Practical Guide for Counselling the Gifted in a School Setting,* edited by J. Van Tassel-Baska (Council for Exceptional Children, 1983), Reston, Virginia.

Tannenbaum, A. J. *Gifted Children: Psychological and Educational Perspectives.* New York: Macmillan, 1983.

Whitmore, Joanne R. "The Potency of Gifted Education in American Schools." *Greentree Quarterly*, 1.1 (Fall 1983).

Whitmore, Joanne R. *Giftedness, Conflict, and Underachievement.* Boston: Allyn & Bacon, 1980.

Webb, James T.; Meckstroth, E. A.; and Tolan, S. S. *Guiding the Gifted Child: A Practical Source for Parents and Teachers.* Ohio Psychology Pub. Co., 1982.

2

Identity:
Self and Others

"It is likely that self-esteem both enhances and is enhanced by successes in various areas." (Janos et al., 1985).

Introduction

Psychologists have recognized for many decades that self-identity lies at the core of the human personality and the process of maturation. The biggest problem has been identifying the various types and components of self-identity. It is perhaps best to start with a comprehensive definition that uses the term self-concept interchangeably to mean: "all those perceptions which an individual holds to be true regarding his or her personal existence." (Purkey et al., 1984)

The acquisition of this self-concept begins at the earliest period in one's life. In fact, most of these perceptions that constitute the total image are acquired and relatively stable by the age of formal schooling. The complexity of this growth and development is expressed in the construct of the "general" self-concept proposed by Kash and Borich (1978).

They argue that five interactive, interrelated, and interdependent senses of self result from an individual's interaction with other persons and the external environment. There is always an incompleteness in this process; the broken lines of the circles in this figure attempt to express that incompleteness.

General Self-Concept: (Senses of:)

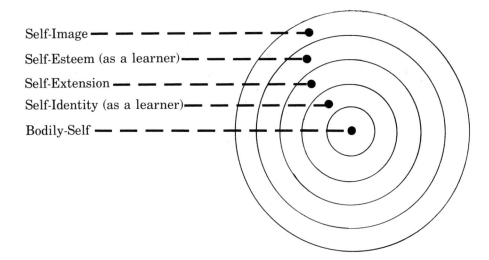

Self-Image
Self-Esteem (as a learner)
Self-Extension
Self-Identity (as a learner)
Bodily-Self

Source: M. Kash and G. Borich, *Teacher Behavior and Pupil Self-Concept* (Reading, MA: Addison-Wesley, 1978), p. 23. ©Addison-Wesley. Reproduced by permission of the publishers.

Within the sub-systems of the general self-concept, Purkey and others (1985) remind us that situation-specific self-images such as the *Self-concept as learner* are extremely important and tend to be underestimated in the general self-concept research. "Students' perceptions of themselves as learners apparently serve as personal guidance systems in directing their behaviour in school. This aspect of self-concept theory plays a critical role in determining students' academic performances." (Purkey et al., 1985, p. 3)

For the gifted student within the context of schooling, ages 8 to 14, his/her self-concept as learner is primarily influenced by two continuously evolving senses, namely (1) a sense of *SELF-IDENTITY*, and (2) a sense of *SELF-ESTEEM*. The first refers to the types of personal relationships involved and the second refers to degree of affirmation or recognition received.

Self-Identity

The sense of self-identity is a psychological construct that represents the sense of self in relation to or affiliation with others. As others interpret and respond to the learner, the self-identity construct evolves. Thus, the quality of the relationships to parents, peers, and teachers as significant others is crucial. Since the gifted learner is emotionally developing at about the same rate as all other peers and yet is considerably advanced cognitively, it is very important that appropriate opportunities exist for:

- A variety of challenging social memberships
- Acquiring a sense of "belonging" or affiliation with a variety of groupings (homogeneous and heterogeneous) of age, interests, and abilities;
- In-school group work, valuing exercises, and individual guidance and consultation; and role-taking;
- Strong role-modeling by teachers and significant others who are aware and sensitive to self-identity needs;
- Parental awareness and support at home and for school efforts to enhance the learner's self-identity.

Although the research results of studies of self-concept and the gifted learner are mixed (Kolloff & Feldhusen, 1984), the implications tend to favor stronger psychosocial support in all of the varied curricular programs. (Janos et al., 1985)

Self-Esteem

The sense of self-esteem is that psychological construct which represents the sum of all the valued *affirmation* or *recognition* experienced by the learner. There is normally sufficient recognition of academic achievements through the competitive rewards system, but the expression of values demonstrating altruism, compassion, social concern may be under-affirmed (Ehrlich, 1982). With the gifted learners heightened sense of societal values and concerns — for example, concerns about nuclear destruction, starvation, population imbalances, environmental protection, and political in-

16

justices — there is a parallel need to affirm those concerns by cultivating a sense of "ownership" in problem solving and other classroom activities.

Society usually expects that the gifted learner will be in a position of leadership once they achieve adulthood and a career. Certainly self-esteem is a powerful component in the acquisition and exercise of leadership. It is imperative that the leader feel strongly confident and comfortable with self in order to achieve tasks at the optimal level of personal functioning.

Teachers can enhance and assure healthy growth in self-esteem by observing consistently the following practices:

- Structure for cooperative learning activities (Johnson et al. 1984);
- Stress individual improvement as the basis for competitive activities;
- Direct praise and criticism to specific aspects of pupil performance;
- Promote the acquisition and use of evaluative skills, e.g., self-reports, group assessments;
- Participation in the establishment of norms or standards used for evaluating products and performance expected in learning;
- Recognition and affirmation of the learners' presence, participation, responses, and performance;
- Use of recommended instructional materials and resources directed to the enhancement of various "senses of the self," for example, Borba (1980-82), Canfield (1976), Dinkmeyer (1980), Purkey and Novak (1984), and Stone and Dillehunt (1978).

The whole process is aptly summarized in the 1983 publication of the Alberta government in the following statement:

"Gifted and talented pupils need time and opportunity to develop with their social peers as well as with their mental peers. The gifted child needs to learn age-appropriate behaviours and develop social acumen. Intellectual development must not ignore physical, emotional, and social development." (Alberta Education, 1983)

References

Alberta Education. *Educating Gifted and Talented Pupils in Alberta.* Planning Service Branch, Alberta Education, 1983.

Borba, Michell and Craig. *Self-Esteem: A Classroom Affair.* Vols. 1 & 2. Minneapolis, Minnesota: Winston Press, 1980 and 1982.

Canfield, Jack, and Wells, Harold S. *100 Ways to Enhance Self-Concept in the Classroom: A Handbook for Teachers and Parents.* New York: Prentice-Hall, 1976.

Clemes, Harris, and Bean, Reynold. *How To Teach Children Responsibility.* San Jose, Ca.: Enrich; Division Ohaus, 1980.

Dinkmeyer, Donald, and Losoncy, Lewis, E. *The Encouragement Book: Becoming a Positive Person.* Englewood Cliffs, N.J.: Prentice-Hall, Spectrum Bk, 1980.

Educational Leadership, 34:7 (April 1982),pp. 484-527.

Ehrlich, V. Z. *Gifted Children: A Guide for Parents and Teachers.* New York: Prentice-Hall, 1982.

Fynn, *Mister God, This Is Anna.* New York: Fontana/Collins, 1974.

Galbraith, Judy. *The Gifted Kids Survival Guide.* Minneapolis, Minnesota: Wetherall Publishing, 1983.

Ginsberg, Gina, and Harrison, Charles. *How to Help Your Gifted Child.* New York: Simon & Schuster, 1977.

Janos, P.: Fung, H.; and Robinson, N. "Self-Concept, Self-Esteem, and Peer Relations among Gifted Children Who Feel 'Different', " *Gifted Child Quarterly,* 29:2 (Spring 1985), pp. 78-82.

Johnson, David; Johnson, Roger; Holubec, Edythe; and Roy, P. *Circles of Learning: Cooperation in the Classroom.* Alexandria, VA: Association for Supervision and Curriculum Development, 1984.

Kash, Marilynn, and Borich, Gary D. *Teacher Behavior and Pupil Self-Concept.* Reading, M.A: Addison-Wesley Publishing Co., 1978.

Kerr, Barbara A. *Smart Girls, Gifted Women.* Columbus, OH.: Ohio Psychology Publishing Company, 1985.

Khatena, Joe. *The Creatively Gifted Child.* New York: Vantage Press, Inc., 1978.

Purkey, William. *Self-concept and School Achievement.* Englewood Cliffs, N.J.: Prentice-Hall, 1970.

Purkey, William W., and Novak, John. *Inviting School Success: A Self-Concept Approach to Teaching and Learning.* 2nd ed. Belmont, CA: Wadsworth Publishers, 1984.

Stone, Karen, and Dillehunt, Harold Q. *Self-Science: The Subject Is Me.* Santa Monica, CA: Goodyear Publishing Co., 1978.

Tannenbaum, Abraham J. *Gifted Children.* New York: Macmillan Publishing Co. Inc., 1983.

Personal Inventory

Purpose: • **To give students an opportunity to express opinions**
• **To react honestly to personal questions**
• **To encourage respect for individuals**

This exercise may be given in September to help the teacher become familiar with his or her students. If children wish to read information aloud, it will help them to learn about each other. Children should be informed at the beginning that they are not required to answer all questions.

ME

Name:_____ Birthday:_____

DAY   MONTH   YEAR

Address: _____ Present Age: _____

Telephone Number: _____

Father's Name: _____ Occupation: _____

Mother's Name:_____ Occupation:_____

No.of Brothers: _____ Ages: _____ No. of Sisters: _____ Ages: _____

1. How do you spend your spare time?_____

_____

2. What did you do during the summer vacation? _____

_____

3. Do you enjoy school? _____ Why?/Why not? _____

_____

4. (a) How much time per day do you spend reading? _____

(hours per day)

(b) Name your favorite book _____

poem _____

5. Which of the following do you read? _____ Newspaper _____ Books

   _____ Magazines _____ Journals _____ Other.

6. What game do you enjoy most? State a reason for this preference.

   _____

7. What is your favorite saying? _____

8. What sports do you appreciate? _____

   participate in? _____

9. Do you enjoy travelling? _____

   Why?/Why not? _____

10. Name some of the places you have visited. _____

    _____

11. Assume that a person has unlimited resources. Suggest three places, throughout the world, this person would visit.

    _____

12. What place in the world would you like to visit most? Give reasons for your choice. _____

13. (a) How much time per day do you spend watching television?

    _____

    (b) What is your favorite television program?

    _____

14. (a) Who is your favorite author? _____

    sports figure? _____

    TV personality? _____

    actor or actress? _____

    world leader? _____

    politician? _____

(b) Why do you admire or respect these people? _____

_____

15. (a) Describe yourself in a paragraph.
    (b) Describe yourself in relation to your family.
    (c) What activities do you share or do with your family?
    (d) Draw a picture of you and your family.

16. What are your expectations for this school year?

_____

17. What do you plan to do to make these expectations become a reality?

_____

18. Of what personal achievement or goal are you most proud?

_____

19. If you could ask one question on any topic, and get a complete answer, what would that question be? Write it.

_____

This exercise is an extension of the previous "Me" inventory. The following is less biographical but more likely to provoke creative and imaginative responses.

"Here's Looking at You Kid"

1. I am happiest when _____

2. I like to think about_____

3. My favorite T-shirt says _____

4. My favorite mascot is _____

5. My favorite saying is _____

6. My favorite autograph is that of_____

7. Some of my interests include _____

8. The person I most admire and respect is _____

9. My first world record will be _____

10. My first book will be dedicated to _____

11. My major accomplishment will be in the field of _____

12. I like my name because_____

13. I am enthusiastic when _____

14. I like to dream about _____

Accept: God, give us grace to accept with serenity the things
that cannot be changed, courage to change the things
that should be changed, and the wisdom to distinguish
the one from the other.

Reinhold Niedohn, *The Serenity Prayer,* 1943

Accept Me

Purpose: • To help children come to terms with their identity
• To encourage open-mindedness and respect for individuals

Discuss the following poem in terms of content and related student experiences. If the students have studied some poetry, it might be worthwhile to consider the form used to express feeling.

> accept me
>   for what I am
> appreciate me
>   as myself
> I am not perfect
>   it doesn't worry me
>   I have many failings
> but I am unique
>   a one-of-a-kind me
> and that is something to be proud of
>   I can change
>   let me do the changing though
> for I will be responsible for the
>   mistakes
>   I make
>   and the accomplishments I achieve
> I want to be the way I am
>   that is my decision
> and if you can't see that
>   then don't blind me
>   with what
>   YOU THINK
>   I should be
> for I am me
>   and nothing else.

Ann Bach, in *Step to the Music You Hear,* vol. 2, edited by Susan Polis Schutz, 1975. Blue Mountain Arts Inc., P. O. Box 4549, Boulder Co. 80302.

To direct discussion, use the following questions:

1. How do you define yourself as an individual?
2. (a) Are there aspects of your personality or life-style that people want you to change? Name them.

(b)   What are the aspects or tendencies which *you* wish to change?

(c)   What can you do to change these habits or tendencies? How can you maintain important aspects of your character or thinking patterns in spite of outside influences?

3.   (a)   How can we develop ways to understand ourselves better?*

(b)   Knowing yourself helps form a basis for understanding others. Why is this true?

(An Example of a Student's Poem)

Images

When I look in the water,
A girl looks up at me,
Large eyes, a nose, and dark brown hair,
And a smile I'm pleased to see.

I wink, she winks,
We play a pleasant game.
Where I move, and what I do,
She does the very same.

I hit the water with my stick,
The face soon disappears.
A new face comes with ugly eyes,
And horrid big fat ears.

I see the pools of water,
Still spinning round and round.
And then I see that smiling face,
Has returned without a sound.

I sit and say hello,
But no one answers me.
I know why they don't because,
An image is all I see.

Kirsti Weeks,
Grade 6,
Ottawa, Ontario.

---

* Explain to children that "understanding" ourselves can include recognizing character traits, strengths, weaknesses, the ability to cope, and willingness to change. Biographies can be an excellent resource for the gifted child since they help us understand ourselves through the motivations, quests, experiences, and failures of other gifted/talented persons.

Open-Ended Sentences

Purpose: • **To promote self-awareness and understanding**
• **To encourage an honest reaction to ideas in print**
•**To encourage adherence to one's principles**

This exercise may be used to help children express, understand, and explain their feelings. Teachers may add ideas or alter them according to the needs of their students. Giving students a chance to express thoughts verbally or in written form can often be helpful to both student and teacher.

Today, I think.......

1. Today I feel.......
2. I enjoy.......
3. I am.......
4. I wish.......
5. I feel.......
6. My peers think.......
7. I think school is.......
8. I enjoy reading.......
9. I hope adults.......
10. The things I like best.......
11. Something I'd like to tell my teacher is.......
12. People I trust.......
13. The best thing.......
14. When I dislike something I've done.......
15. When I like something I've done.......
16. I am very happy that.......
17. I would like to become.......
18. I wish my family.......
19. Someday I hope.......
20. Five adjectives that describe me are.......
21. I liked listening to.......
22. I liked playing.......
23. I enjoy discussing.......
24. I would like to do research on.......

Sample Answers to Open-Ended Sentences

1. Today I feel very tired because last night I stayed up until half-past ten.
2. I enjoy swimming in a lake or a pool, and just relaxing.
3. I am unhappy when I see animals that are unhappy.
4. I wish my teacher in grade 7 could be just like Mrs. Dixon.
5. I feel good when I see animals being treated kindly.
6. My peers think I am a good artist. (I don't really think so.)

7. I think school is worthwhile, because it would be a terrible world if people weren't educated.
8. I enjoy reading about animals and I also like mysteries.
9. I hope adults will stop treating kids like doormats.
10. The thing I like best about my class is that it is nice and big and my classmates are kind.
11. Something I'd like to tell my teacher is.......

   NOTE: Emily chose not to complete this statement. Her wishes should be respected since the questions or open-ended sentences are of a personal nature.
12. People I trust are the people I think are the most important people in my life.
13. The best thing that could happen to me would be if I could have wings and fly.
14. When I dislike something I've done, I try to correct it.
15. When I like something I've done, I try to remember how I did it and try to use the same method in other matters.
16. I am very happy that I live in such a nice, kind family.
17. I would like to become a cartoonist when I grow up.
18. I wish my family knew how much I enjoy going to school.
19. Someday I hope that all prejudice will be gone, and all people will be equal.
20. Five adjectives that describe me are: "stubborn, funny, active, understanding, and sometimes lazy."
21. I liked listening to *Jacob Two-Two Meets the Hooded Fang* because it was funny and showed that children are equal.
22. I liked playing "Imaginery Playmate."
23. I enjoy discussing ways of dealing with conflict.
24. I would like to do research on holography.

Emily Lye,
Grade 5, Ottawa, Ontario.

ME

Alone and angry
Trying to be
Someone I'm not
That describes me.

Trying to fit in
Where no one has want
Ignoring in tears
their teases and taunts.

Finding new friends
Is harder for me
Being who I am
Not who I want to be.

Everyone has problems
I shouldn't complain
I've so much to lose
And so much to gain.

I've found and I've lost
A few friends along the way
Some have thought to leave
Some, to stay.

I'm standing at crossroads
Confused, trying to see
Who I am. I have to
Find, and be, me.

Kate Baillie,
Grade 9, Orangeville, Ontario.

Self-Image
"Co-operative Learning"

Purpose:	• To encourage interdependence in the classroom
	• To develop an open-minded attitude and a respect for human dignity

One of our most important tasks as teachers is to teach children to care for each other. The concept we know as childhood only came into existence in the nineteenth century with William Wordsworth being a primary exponent. Our expectations for children are often too limited and we dismiss acts of folly or cruelty as the mere acts of children or adolescents. Our demands on children must be more than minimal. Children must not be allowed to act in a selfish or callous manner but taught to help and care for each other as well as themselves.

Our classrooms should be structured to encourage humane treatment from child to child. We thus make the world possible for every child and consciously teach no child that the world revolves around him or her. This philosophy echoes U. Thant's comments in the '60s when he stated that we shall all pay the price if we do not assume responsibility for each other.

We shall outline one method which can be used to emphasize caring in the classroom:

(a) During the first few weeks of school gather as many pieces of writing as possible from the students; talk to them individually; note quality and quantity of participation in groups discussions; test students objectively. These subjective and objective evaluations allow the teacher to determine the literacy rate of students and to rank them.

(b) Rank all students in class. Divide the class into three sections and select groups from these sections. Thirty-six students — rank number 1 to 36.

Sections		Groups
a. # 1-12	#1,13,25	7,19,31
b. #13-24	#2,14,26	8,20,32
c. #25-36	#3,15,27	9,21,33
	#4,16,28	10,22,34
	#5,17,29	11,23,25
	#6,18,30	12,24,36

(c) Group children by continuously placing the top child from each section in a group of three.* Since groups must consist of both sexes, rearrange groups only to achieve this end. Inform children that groups are absolutely inflexible. "You belong to each other and must assume responsibility for each other."

(d) Further explain the co-operative system to the students. "An important dimension of this class is to share the responsibility for each other's learning. In order to do this, we will start with each person sharing responsibility and caring for two other people in particular. Your satisfaction depends on theirs and vice versa. To teach others is to learn oneself." Learning should be more successful since humans can seldom escape the unremitting pressure of their peers.

(e) *Group Marks*
One piece of written work shall be expected from each child on a weekly basis. This writing shall be proofread and initialled by the two other members of your group. A group mark shall be assigned for this submission only. In this there will be many opportunities to share responsibility for each other and learn to think well of ourselves and others.

Related Reading

For an excellent article on "Caring," read Urie Bronfenbrenner, "Our Schools Need a Curriculum for Caring," *Instructor*, February, 1979.

For further information on the historical and sociological aspects of childhood, refer to Phillippe Ariès, *Centuries of Childhood: A Social History of Family Life*. (New York: Random House, 1965).

For additional information on "co-operative learning", see D. W. Johnson and F. Johnson, *Joining Together: Group Theory and Group Skills*, 2nd ed. (Englewood Cliffs, N.J.: Prentice-Hall, 1982).

---

* This ranking system works since the gap between the children isn't as great as it would be if we placed the most literate child (#1) with the least literate child (#36). We must attempt to avoid condescension or patronage. The difference must be bridgeable.

Self-Image

Charlotte's Web: An Excerpt

This excerpt from *Charlotte's Web* should be read silently by students, after which the teacher may read it aloud and use it as a starting point for a discussion on individual differences. This excerpt lends itself to characterization. Children may assign a particular trait to one of the characters and use textual evidence to support the characterization.

*   *   *

"   Where's Papa going with the ax? said Fern to her mother as they were setting the table for breakfast.

"Out to the hoghouse," replied Mrs. Arable. "Some pigs were born last night."

"I don't see why he needs an ax," continued Fern, who was only eight.

"Well," said her mother, "one of the pigs is a runt. It's very small and weak, and it will never amount to anything. So your father has decided to do away with it."

"Do AWAY with it?" shrieked Fern. "You mean KILL it? Just because it's smaller than the others?"

Mrs. Arable put a pitcher of cream on the table. "Don't yell, Fern!" she said. "Your father is right. The pig would probably die anyway."

Fern pushed a chair out of the way and ran outdoors. The grass was wet and the earth smelled of springtime. Fern's sneakers were sopping by the time she caught up with her father.

"Please don't kill it!" she sobbed. "It's unfair."

Mr. Arable stopped walking. "Fern," he said gently, "you will have to learn to control yourself."

"Control myself?" yelled Fern. "This is a matter of life and death and you talk about CONTROLLING myself." Tears ran down her cheeks and she took hold of the ax and tried to pull it out of her father's hand.

"Fern," said Mr. Arable, "I know more about raising a litter of pigs than you do. A weakling makes trouble. Now run along!"

"But it's unfair," cried Fern. "The pig couldn't help being born small, could it? If I had been very small at birth, would you have killed ME?"

Mr. Arable smiled. "Certainly not," he said, looking down at his daughter with love. "But this is different. A little girl is one thing, a little runty pig is another."

"I see no difference," replied Fern, still hanging onto the ax. "This is the most terrible case of injustice I ever heard of."

A queer look came over John Arable's face. He seemed almost ready to cry himself.

"All right," he said. "you go back to the house and I will bring the runt when I come in. I'll let you start it on a bottle, like a baby. Then you'll see what trouble a pig can be."

When Mr. Arable returned to the house half an hour later, he carried a carton under his arm. Fern was upstairs changing her sneakers. The kitchen table was set for breakfast, and the room smelled of coffee, bacon, damp plaster, and wood smoke from the stove.

"Put it on her chair!" said Mrs. Arable. Mr. Arable set the carton down at Fern's place. Then he walked to the sink and washed his hands and dried them on the roller towel.

Fern came slowly down the stairs. Her eyes were red from crying. As she approached her chair, the carton wobbled, and there was a scratching noise. Fern looked at her father. Then she lifted the lid of the carton. There, inside, looking up at her, was the newborn pig. It was a white one. The morning light shone through its ears, turning them pink.

"He's yours," said Mr. Arable. "Saved from an untimely death. And may the good Lord forgive me for this foolishness."

Fern couldn't take her eyes off the tiny pig. "Oh," she whispered. "Oh, look at him! He's absolutely perfect."

She closed the carton carefully. First she kissed her father, then she kissed her mother. Then she opened the lid again, lifting the pig out, and held it against her cheek. At this moment her brother Avery came into the room. Avery was ten. He was heavily armed — an air rifle in one hand, a wooden dagger in the other.

"What's that?" he demanded. "What's Fern got?"

"She's got a guest for breakfast," said Mrs. Arable. "Wash your hands and face, Avery!"

"Let's see it!" said Avery, setting his gun down. "You call that miserable thing a pig? That's a fine specimen of a pig — its no bigger than a white rat."

"Wash up and eat your breakfast, Avery!" said his mother. "The school bus will be along in half an hour."

"Can I have a pig too, Pop?" asked Avery.

"No, I only distribute pigs to early risers," said Mr. Arable. "Fern was up at daylight, trying to rid the world of injustice. As a result, she now has a pig. It just shows what can happen if a person gets out of bed promptly. Let's eat!"

Charlotte's Web — Classroom Discussion

> **Purpose:** • To present an example of situational con-
> flict and personal crisis which serves as a
> model for students
> • To encourage involvement and adherence
> to principles

1. After reading the excerpt, write impressions of each of the following characters: Fern Arable, Mr. Arable, Mrs. Arable, and Avery Arable. Include a quotation to support your characterization.

2. Use the text as the basis for a script. Dramatize the "before breakfast" scene.

3. Discuss the excerpt on three levels: (i) facts, (ii) concepts, and (iii) values.

   Facts:
   (a) Why is Fern upset with her father?
   (b) What is a runt?
   (c) How does Fern save the runt?
   (d) How does Fern care for the pig?
   (e) How does Avery react to the situation?

   Concepts:
   (a) What is E. B. White saying to us in this excerpt?
   (b) (i) Was Fern's argument practical? Why/Why not?
        (ii) What does it tell you about Fern?
   (c) How would you describe "jealousy"?

   Values:
   (a) Tell classmates about a time when you disputed a decision. What reasons did you give? Were your reasons valid? Write a story based on this event.

   (b) (i) Have you ever been jealous? Did you dislike the feelings associated with jealousy? How did you handle the feelings?

       (ii) How can you tell when people are jealous of you? What should you do? Do you care enough to help people overcome feelings like jealousy? How do feelings of jealousy compare with feelings of inadequacy?

Charlotte's Web — Samples of Characterization

1. Fern Arable: kind and considerate:
"But it's unfair" in reference to killing the runt.

animal lover:

''he's perfect'' — referring to the pig.

2. **Avery Arable:**   jealous:

''You call that miserable thing a pig?''

''Could I have one too?'' — in reference to the pig.

mean:

''it's no bigger than a white rat'' — trying to make Fern unhappy with the pig.

3. **Mr. Arable:**   strict — killing the runt.

a kind Father:

''He's yours to keep'' — in reference to the pig.

4. **Mrs. Arable:**   kind:

''Avery, go wash your hands and face'' — so that he could not go on hurting Fern's feelings.

Anthony Duncker,
Grade 4,
Ottawa, Ontario.

On Being Gifted

Scorned, no, feared
Which?
Highly motivated
Always seeking
Must know, must know
No time to be social
Too much time to be social
Outcasts, leaders
The girl in the front row.
Confusion
Decisions, problems
Easily solved?
Always ahead?
Sometimes behind.

Abstract, ingenious
Faster, faster
Speed up
Hunger for knowledge
Day dreamers
Shy, extrovert
Strong?
Frustration
Why can't I
I must, I must
Lonely.
Feelings
Help! need someone!
Accept
Understand
A whole person.

Kate Armstrong,
Grade 10,
Orangeville, Ontario.

Identity Study

Preparation Exercise for Essay on Self-Identity

Purpose: • To develop a concept of identity
• To encourage self-awareness among students

From this list of various things that students feel are important, prioritize the things that are *very important* to you. Expand on *three of the most important choices.*

1. Being a winner in games.
2. Having lots of spending money.
3. Being able to bring friends into my home.
4. Being able to have my own reading material and audio tapes.
5. Doing well in academic subjects.
6. Being at ease with my friends, associates, and classmates.
7. Being able to travel to new places.
8. Having friends and kindred spirits.
9. Having many hobbies.
10. Having my own space and time to be alone.
11. Being able to select the clothes I want and being able to afford them.
12. Having my own stereo system.
13. Having my own computer.
14. Getting along well with my family.

In a paragraph, indicate your most important choice and tell why you made it.

_____

_____

_____

_____

_____

_____

_____

Identity Study

Characteristics and Traits of Humans

Purpose:	• To provide children with vocabulary with which they may describe themselves and others. • To increase awareness of characterization in reading.

Brainstorm to develop this list of characteristics *or* allow groups to develop lists. Bring groups together and record items on experience on chart paper. This exercise helps the student to prepare to write an essay on self-identity.

Sample List

1. Stubborn/Malleable
2. Joiner/Aloof
3. Silly/Sensible
4. Likeable/Unpopular
5. Humorous/Serious
6. Dependable/Unreliable
7. Graceful/Awkward
8. Honest/Fabricator
9. Loyal/Disloyal
10. Intelligent/Dull
11. Successful/Failure
12. Unique/Uniform
13. Dull/Scintillating
14. Garrulous/Pensive
15. Imaginative/Conforming
16. Creative/Plodding
17. Stingy/Generous
18. Ambitious/Carefree
19. Mean/Gentle
20. Sensitive/Unfeeling
21. Cruel/Caring
22. Courageous/Timid
23. Serious/Light-Hearted
24. Nervous/Relaxed
25. Independent/Dependent
26. Considerate/Inconsiderate
27. Mischievous/Obedient
28. Angelic/Satanic
29. Practical/Illogical
30. Complaining/Reticent
31. Eager/Reluctant
32. Willing/Unwilling
33. Capable/Incapable
34. Artistic/Concrete
35. Obedient/Daring
36. Greedy/Philanthropic
37. Helpful/Selfish
38. Devious/Up-front
39. Dignified/Dishevelled
40. Confident/Insecure
41. Ignorant/Learned
42. Envious/Accepting
43. Evil/Innocent
44. Forgetful/Organized
45. Courteous/Disrespectful
46. Worrisome/Carefree
47. Friendly/Hostile
48. Destructive/Constructive
49. Dreamy/Realist
50. Angry/Jovial
51. Judicious/Malevolent
52. Shy/Popular
53. Selfish/Altruistic
54. Emotional/Rational
55. Sensible/Foolish
56. Individualistic/Communal
57. Prudent/Careless
58. Wise/Inexperienced
59. Forgiving/Vengeful

Sharene Baird,
Grade 6, Carleton Place, Ontario.

Self-Identity Essay

Purpose:	• To help children understand themselves and their identity within a societal context
	• To further the personal development of each child

Following circle discussions, exercises, and reading on the theme of "self-image" or identity, students are instructed to write an identity essay.

The assignment may be structured according to student needs. Structured and unstructured assignments are both effective. A traditional "autobiography" exercise may be used as an alternative.

A sample essay and an explanation of headings are required to help students write a meaningful essay.

Outline for "Identity Essay" is as follows:

I. **Knowledge of Outer Self**
   (i)   Physical appearance
   (ii) Physical skills
   (iii) Sexual Image
   (iv) Age

II. **Knowledge of Inner Self**
   (i)   Personality traits
   (ii) Characteristics
   (iii) Values

III. **Social Relationships**
   (i)   Teachers
   (ii) Friends
   (iii) Family

IV. **Knowledge of Cultural Setting**
   (i)   Role of Religion
   (ii) National origin
   (iii) Travels
   (iv) Residences

V. **Influence of Past Experiences**
   (i)   Personal control
   (ii) Social control

VI. **Uniqueness as an Individual**
   (i)   Interests
   (ii) Hobbies
   (iii) Ambitions

Adapted from Marguerite Burke, *Identity in a Canadian Urban Community,* Project Canada West, Brunskill Subproject, Saskatoon, Saskatchewan, 1972.

Self-Identity Essay: Sample I

Knowledge of Outer Self

My name is Alexander Hay and at the present time I am living on Carling Avenue. I have medium brown hair, blue eyes, and a fair complexion. I am male, and I think this makes a great difference to my life. For instance, my sister, because of this, assumes I enjoy living in a messy room. I am eleven and a half years old.

Knowledge of Inner Self

I think that I am ambitious. At the moment, I would very much like to become a doctor.

I am excitable, intelligent, attentive, and kind (most of the time). I try always to remain happy. My sister calls me "angelic" or "angel face" but this is not true at all.

I value above all my family and next to them, relations and friends.

I have always valued truth and honesty above all other virtues, but once, I did not manage.

I was in South Africa at the time and Christmas shopping for my brothers and sister. I found a small tea set that I thought Lyndal would like. It had two price labels on it, one 50¢ and the other R 1.50. Before I knew what was happening, I had ripped off the more valuable price tag and paid 50¢ for the tea set. I then joined my brothers and sister, who were elsewhere in the store. My first inclination was to just run home and forget all about it, but my conscience weighed heavily on me and just as we were leaving the shop, I slipped one Rand (that is the kind of money they use in South Africa) and ran from the shop as quickly as I could. Upon reaching my Grandfather's house, at which we were staying, I felt quite ill and soon developed a mild case of German measles.

Social Relationships

I believe that to have a good relationship with anyone you must trust and like them. I think that trusting a friend is vital or else that person is not a real friend, but just "the boy or girl next door."

I am very close to all of my family although I fight a lot with my brothers and sister. I have many friends in South Africa, as well as in Scotland and Canada.

Knowledge of Cultural Settings

I am Presbyterian and my religion plays a great part in my life. I enjoy going to Church and believe in God as an individual.

National Origin

My Grandfather (on my father's side) came from Scotland to South Africa when he was thirty years old. He lived in Johannesburg and there my father was born.

On my mother's side, my Grandfather's father came from Belfast, Ireland, to Johannesburg, South Africa, and my Grandfather was born there. My mother was born in a small town in the Transvaal, called Heidelberg.

Influence of Past Experiences

I think that I have good personal control, and social control, and I don't have a quick temper. I like making friends and enjoy being with other people, although I'm shy at meeting new children.

Uniqueness as an Individual

When I grow up I would like to become a doctor.

My sister and I own a small electric train set, consisting of one engine, three cars, a level crossing, a small house set-up, and several feet of track. I would like to expand this. I enjoy operating it.

I like horseback-riding very much and also enjoy swimming, tobogganning, skating, table-tennis and canoeing.

Alex Hay,
Grade 6, Ottawa, Ontario.

*　　　　　*　　　　　*

Self-Identity Essay: Sample II

Knowledge of Outer Self

My name is Alexandra Mathewson. My parents didn't give me a middle name because my middle name would be Ruby, after my grandmother and my parents didn't like that idea.

I have blonde hair and a fair complexion. I have blue eyes and in different light the color of them can vary from steel grey to china blue. My feet are quite big for my age, I can fit into my sister's shoes, and she's 21!

I normally have a good posture and I'm quite thin. My facial expression is normally serious.

I don't like most running sports but I do like swimming. I got my star three swimming badge but I don't think I deserve it.

I also like climbing trees and hills, I like riding my bike and dancing (most kinds). I like doing delicate work (with my hands) like painting, drawing, and model making.

I am a girl and I think I'm lucky for it. For instance I enjoy dressing up in pretty clothes but sometimes they're pretty uncomfortable. So I also can wear jeans and overalls which are comfortable. But although boys could wear dresses they probably wouldn't anyway.

I am 10 years old but sometimes I wish I could be older. The reason is that, other than classmates, I normally play with older people and when I tell them I'm ten they give me a weird look like "You're ten?" which makes me feel embarrassed. I think that ten is a nice year after all and I don't know what 11, 12, 13, . . . will be like.

Knowledge of Inner Self

I normally try to be a happy and friendly person. I tend to go along with what the majority wants although I do have my own personal opinions. Quite often I worry about lots of things (I blow things all out of proportion). I am pretty smart and I can learn most things fast.

I am an honest and trustworthy person. Mostly the only lies I tell are little white lies. I'm a sensitive person, for example, when my mother or sisters are crying or upset, I get upset too. I put lots of things off and sometimes I can be very lazy.

I value lots of things, most of which come from nature. I value the beauty of nature and wildlife. I also value good relationships between families and friends (trust, respect, understanding). I value being a Canadian because Canada has lots of beautiful places.

Social Relationships

I can learn to like most teachers even if I hate the subject. I can talk honestly and openly with almost all teachers. I think that a teacher should be honest and fair (like Mrs. Dixon).

I have many friends in Canada although I only have one best friend who is in England and I'm going to see her next summer. I like having lots of friends but only one best friend. I think a friend should be fun to be with and nice.

I feel I'm an important part of my family because I'm a ''peacemaker'' which means I try to help people who are upset. I go to my mother for help when I need it. I like being in my family because we have funny times but sometimes our family gets too sarcastic and I don't like that.

Knowledge of Cultural Setting

I am Protestant. I enjoy going to church but our family doesn't go too often because we're in the country on weekends. I do believe in God but not according to the Bible.

Right now both my mother and my father are Canadian but once my mother was American. She became Canadian by living in Canada for a certain amount of time.

My father descended from Vikings and my mother descended from Irish and Scottish (which was what Vikings descended from).

I've been on many trips some of which include Austria, Switzerland, France, Italy, Grand Canary Islands and I am going to Germany and England this summer. I enjoy travelling with my family. I've learnt a lot.

I have lived in three main places. Germany, I lived there four years. England, I lived there one year. Canada, I've lived here five years. All of the places I have lived were because of my father's work.

Influence of Past Experiences

''I wasn't too sure what Personal Control and Social Control meant so I wrote my interpretation of it. . . ''

Normally my family lets me decide what I want to do by myself. Sometimes my mother and father decide what to do for me (if necessary). I normally find that my decisions are right.

I normally do what is best for me, especially if it will change my life. For instance, if everyone is going to boarding school or quitting school because that's the ''in thing'' I probably would do what suits me at the moment.

Uniqueness as an Individual

My ''interests'' are games, and television for indoors. I also like reading but I have been corrupted by television. I love most animals for their beauty.

Alixe Matthewson,
Grade 5, Ottawa, Ontario.

Identity Study

Essay on "Kindred Spirits"

> Purpose: • To assist the student in recognizing self-identity and the identities of members of any peer group (i.e. intellectual peers, social peers)

The teacher could begin this exercise by discussing the concept of "kindred spirits", referring specifically to the characters Diana and Anne from Lucy Maude Montgomery's classic novel, *Anne of Green Gables.*

From this discussion the idea of special friends, the formation of such friendships, and the mutual benefits of these ideal relationships could then be explored.

The writing process could be initiated if the student were to keep a point form collection of the traits ascribed to his/her "kindred spirit". Reference to specific characteristics and values is essential at this point in the study.

This collection of traits should then be organized into a cohesive essay illustrating the concept of "kindred spirits".

Identity Study

Sample of an Essay on "Kindred Spirits"

My Kindred Spirit

My kindred spirit, first of all, does not have to be like me. After all, having a special friend who is exactly like me would be awfully boring, wouldn't it?

A person who doesn't like jokes, or is very serious wouldn't fit in with me. For one thing, I don't think that person would like me, because I do not like to always be serious. My friend should also understand me; not thoroughly, though, because like everyone else, I do have secrets and other personal matters that only me and my family know about. This person should be trustworthy and should trust me. Whether a person is tall, short, chubby or thin makes no difference to me, because what really counts is his or her behavior toward me and toward other people and not the person's physical appearance.

My kindred spirit is my dog, Jill. She is a black poodle, and if anything ever happened to her, I don't know what I'd do. Where I go, she goes, and that's it. The one good thing about dogs is that they can never insult you, or complain or bother you in any way. On the other hand, dogs live in such a silent world, it is probably horrible going through life not being able to express feelings the way humans do.

As I have said, my kindred spirit would have to have a good sense of humor, and would have to have a few things in common, and we should like and do a few things similar, but not everything.

Emily Lye,
Grade 4,
Ottawa, Ontario.

Poem for Discussion I
The Question

1. If I could teach you how to fly
   Or bake an elderberry pie
   Or turn the sidewalk into stars
   Or play new songs on old guitars
   Or if I knew the way to heaven
   The names of night, the taste of seven,
   And owned them all, to keep or lend —
   Would you come and be my friend?

2. You cannot teach me how to fly.
   I love the berries but not the pie
   The sidewalks are for walking on.
   An old guitar has just one song.
   The names of night cannot be known,
   The way to heaven cannot be shown,
   You cannot keep, you cannot lend —
   But still I want you for a friend.

—*Dennis Lee,* Nicholas Knock, and Other People
(Toronto: Macmillan Co. of Canada, 1974), p. 28.

Reprinted by permission of the author.

Probe Questions
1. Do you have a friend? Tell us about one of your friends.
2. What is "friendship"?
3. How does Dennis Lee interpret friendship?
4. What makes a good friend?
5. How might you keep a friend?
6. In your opinion, is it better to have a lot of friends or just a few friends? Does it depend on the individual?
7. When you first came to school, to a club, or to a new neighborhood, how did you make friends?
8. Do you ever make an effort to help someone make friends with your friends?

Collage on Image of Self

```
Purpose:  • To develop a concept of identity
          • To encourage self-awareness among students
```

This activity may be approached in two ways:

(1) Using chart paper and felt markers, have the students outline their body shape. Characteristics that illustrate the student's self-image could be written inside the body shape. Drawings, photographs, or cut-out pictures could be used in a similar manner.
(2) With the aid of an overhead or opaque projector, outline the head of the student and transfer this outline onto dark construction paper. Students could then cut pictures from magazines, or use photographs, which reveal their identity and glue these cuttings onto the construction paper shape.

Upon the completion of either activity each student should be given the opportunity to explain how his/her collage depicts both personality and self-image.

Poem for Discussion II

Don't Dress Your Cat in an Apron

Don't dress your cat in an apron
Just 'cause he's learning to bake.
Don't put your horse in a nightgown
Just 'cause he can't stay awake.
Don't dress your snake in a muu-muu
Just 'cause he's off on a cruise.
Don't dress your whale in galoshes
If she really prefers overshoes.
A person should wear what he wants to
And not just what other folks say.
A person should do what she likes to —
A person's a person that way

—*Dan Greenburg,*
Free To Be You and Me
(Toronto: McGraw-Hill, 1974)

Probe Questions
1. What is the meaning of "conformity"?
2. How can we help others retain their uniqueness?
3. In one sentence, state the meaning of this poem.

Identity Shop Simulation Game

> **Purpose:** • To help the student feel that he/she has unique characteristics and needs
> To develop skill in small group and class discussion

Given the Identity Shop Simulation Game, the student should be able to choose four commodities that he/she wishes to buy. Each student should be able to write four choices.

The student should be able to choose, in cooperation with the group, commodities for each student. He/she must function within the limitations set down by the game. Each student should be able to make one contribution to the classroom discussion.

Given the Identity Shop Simulation Game, the student should be able to contribute to a class discussion in which he/she analyses the group interaction, his/her own identity, and the identity of others. Each student should make one contribution to the class discussion.

The teacher may give each student a copy of the Identity Shop Simulation Game and a sheet of paper (blank) on which he/she will write a choice. When each member of a group has made a choice, the teacher will allot to the group an amount of money. The group is allocated five dollars per student. They are told only the group sum, not the student sum. Students are allowed twenty-five minutes to play the game. When the time is up, each group may comment on its decisions. Students who wish may read their original choices and the group's choice for them.

Probe Questions

(a)   Why did we play this game?
(b)   What does this game have to do with real life?
(c)   What did you learn about your own identity?
(d)   What did you learn about the identity of others in your group?

Instructions for the Students

Identity Shop Simulation Game

1.   Your teacher will assign each of you to a group.
2.   Each of you will be given an advertisement from the Identity Shop.
3.   Read over the advertisement and decide on four commodities that you wish to buy. Write these on the sheet of paper that has been provided.

4. When all members of your group have completed a list of four items, your teacher will tell you how much money your group has to spend.

5. Each group will decide on which commodity they will buy for each student. Purchases must be based on your four original choices. The group may not make your choice for you. They may, however, refuse to buy any item if they cannot afford it. More than one item may be purchased for each student.

6. Decisions must be made by a majority vote. The group may not exceed the amount of money allotted. There is no borrowing, loaning, or credit terms.

7. Each group will appoint a treasurer to keep an account of its money.

8. Each item may be sold only once.

9. Each student must keep a list of the original four items that he/she chose, and a list of what the group bought for him/her.

10. There is a time limit of twenty-five minutes on the game.

11. Money left over may be put in a savings account.

12. Organize your group so that they can make decisions about items that they wish to buy.

I wish I could stay up later.	$4.00	I need to be with people all the time.	$4.00
I wish I wouldn't lose things.	$3.00	I like to wear clothes different from those worn by other boys and girls.	$2.00
I wish I were smaller.	$5.00		
I wish I weren't so clumsy.	$5.00	I like touching the people I care about.	$3.00
I wish I were handsome.	$6.00	I need quiet and personal time.	$4.00
I wish I weren't the eldest in the family.	$5.00	I wish my self-expectations were higher/lower.	$3.00
I wish I were less messy.	$3.00		
I wish I were better organized.	$4.00	I wish I were less sensitive to the feelings of myself and others.	$3.00
I wish I had better writing.	$3.00	I wish I were athletic.	$5.00
I wish I were thinner.	$5.00	I wish I were bigger.	$5.00
I like girls.	$3.00	I wish that I weren't a follower.	$5.00
I am a quiet person.	$1.00		
I wish I had "liberated" attitudes.	$4.00	I wish I were beautiful.	$6.00
My father is the greatest man in the world.	$3.00	I dislike boys	$3.00

I wish I weren't the youngest in the family.	$5.00	My mother is the greatest woman in the world.	$3.00
I hate dresses and skirts.	$2.00	I like to choose clothes similar to those worn by other boys and girls.	$4.00
I wish I could be more pleasant.	$4.00		
I wish I were rich.	$6.00	I wish that people liked me.	$3.00
I feel that I have to succeed in everything I undertake.	$5.00	I wish that my teacher understood me.	$3.00
I like boys.	$3.00	I wish I had lots of money to spend.	$3.00
I am a talkative person.	$1.00	I wish other students would stop teasing me.	$4.00
I believe all people should be free to be themselves.	$4.00	I would like to be a model student.	$3.00

From Marguerite Burke, *Identity in a Canadian Urban Community, Student Resource Book,* Project Canada West, Saskatoon, Saskatchewan, 1973, pp. 3-5.

Factors to Be Considered Following the Game

1. Your group may now comment on its final decisions describing the way that you spend your money.
2. If you wish, you may read off what you originally wanted and what your group bought for you.
3. Why do you suppose that we played this game?
4. What does this game have to do with real life?
5. What determines how you make choices in real life?
6. What did you learn about your own identity?
7. What did you learn about the identity of others in your group?

Why Me?

The question comes unanswered
The truth is hard to see
The answer's not within my reach
But I wish "me" were "we".

Their teases and taunts
Their moans and wants
Their laughs, their jeers
My pain, my tears.

The question comes unanswered
The truth is hard to see
The answer is too far away
The question is: Why me?

Kate Baillie,
Grade 9,
Orangeville, Ontario.

44

Someday

Midnight approaches
The day draws to an end
Far in the distance
You hear a whippoorwill
Calling endlessly
Not only for what it has lost
But for what it never had.

Calling for that one thing
That would make its life complete
That one thing
That ever elusive thing
That someday. . .

Kate Baillie,
Grade 9, Orangeville, Ontario.

Suggested Readings

Clark, Barbara. *Growing Up Gifted.* 2nd ed. Columbus, OH.: Merrill Pub. Co., 1983, chapter 3.

Dinkmeyer, Don, and Lilosoncy, L. *Encouragement Book: Becoming a Positive Person.* Englewood Cliffs, N.J.: Prentice Hall, 1980.

Ehrlich, V. Z. *Gifted Children.* Englewood Cliffs, N.J.: Prentice-Hall Inc., 1982.

Freeman, Joan, ed. *The Psychology of the Gifted Child.* Rexdale, Ont.: John Wiley & Sons, 1985.

Greene, Constance C. *Alexandra the Great.* New York: Dell Publishing Co., Inc., 1982.

Khatena, Joe. *Educational Psychology of the Gifted.* Rexdale, Ont.: John Wiley & Sons, 1982.

Konigsburg, E. L. *From the Mixed-Up Files of Mrs. Basil E. Frankweiler.* Toronto: McClelland and Stewart, 1967.

Lee, Dennis. *Nicholas Knock.* Toronto: Macmillan of Canada, 1974.

McCarthy, Mary Sue. "Self and Other — The Right to a Human Education." In *Human Rights in Canadian Education,* edited by D. Ray and V. D'Oyley. Dubuque, Iowa: Kendall/Hunt Pub. Co., 1983.

Miller, Alice. *The Drama of The Gifted Child.* Lake Station, IN.: Basic Books, 1981.

Paterson, Katherine. *Bridge to Teribithia.* New York: Avon Books, 1977.

Potok, Chaim. *My Name Is Asher Lev.* New York: Ballantine Books, 1972.

Powell, Philip, and Haden, Tony. "The Intellectual & Psychosocial Nature of Extreme Giftedness." *Roeper Review,* 6:3 (February 1984), pp. 131-33.

Salinger, J. D. *Franny & Zooey.* New York: Bantam Books, Inc., 1964.

Shallcross, Doris. *Teaching Creative Behaviour.* Englewood Cliffs, N.J.: Prentice-Hall Inc., 1981.

Shallcross, Doris, and Sisk, Dorothy. *The Growing Person.* Englewood Cliffs, N.J.: Prentice-Hall Inc., 1982.

Vail, Priscilla V. *The World of the Gifted Child.* New York: Penguin, 1980.

Whitmore, Joanne. *Conflict Giftedness and Underachievement.* Boston: Allyn & Bacon Inc., 1981, Chapter 5.

3

Human Rights:
Individual and Social

Introduction

"I HAVE A RIGHT TO:
identify my abilities and to excel,
contribute to society,
learn more in school than I knew last year,
share my knowledge with others,
develop my curiosity and creativity,
apply what I learn through problem solving,
make friends with gifted peers,
contribute to the growth of my peers,
be different from my peers,
respect and learn from others who differ from me,
explore alternatives and to experience consequences,
say how I might be freed from undue anxiety."

(Dirkes, 1983)

While the gifted might justifiably claim all of these individual rights, they must put this within the context of societal rights. Society can also have claims on the individual citizen or member. In fact, fundamental to the lives of all citizens living in societies ruled and established upon democratic principles is the need for a careful balance in the exercise of rights and responsibilities. These are two sides of the same precious coin.

The present generation of youth has perhaps experienced an emphasis on individual rights to the detriment of societal responsibilities. The protection of individuals through both public and private agencies, for example, human rights commissions, is commonplace. We in Canada are particularly fortunate to experience the application of a new Constitution (Constitution Act, 1982) and the early interpretation of its Charter of Rights and Freedoms. The sensitive "equality rights" provision will require many years of judicial interpretation.

It has been suggested (Thompson, 1985) that this new constitution has shifted the significant basis of law from the Parliament to the courts. When the issue of limitations upon one's rights reaches the courts, the government will have to determine through the courts that these limitations "are reasonable limits prescribed by law as can be demonstrably justified in a free and democratic society (#1)."

Unfortunately, there is no mention of corresponding responsibilities. This is where the educational process and any other means will have to speak out. The gifted with their intellectual abilities and increased sensitivity to various social concerns should be encouraged to (a) problem solve, and (b) develop a positive attitude and concern for the common good of the citizenry. This can start with local social concerns and expand outward to the ultimate global and extraterrestrial context.

Gifted students have wonderful opportunities to collect data from many resources, for example, video, newspapers, and microcomputers. The use of public documents can make them realize that the founding generation practised societal equity and living arrangements that required a great degree of self and communal discipline for the sake of the commonweal.

Classroom activities that generate parallel lists of rights and responsibilities, that engage the students in the formation of norms and rules for the management of their school affairs, and that promote field studies and group and individual activities will be attractive to all students but particularly to the precocious.

It is important that students study carefully their nation's constitution, for example, know the fundamental freedoms protected:

(a) freedom of conscience and religion;
(b) freedom of thought, belief, opinion, and expression, including freedom of the press and other media of communication;
(c) freedom of peaceful assembly; and
(d) freedom of association.

However, beyond this, by engaging in experiential activities, for example, mock courts, visits to city and provincial governments, contact of a government representative at various levels, field studies, in-class simulations, student attitudes will also change or develop.

Teachers also have access to helpful resources through current events, government agencies, and published instructional materials in professional magazines and bookstores (Hardy, 1984/85).

References

Dirkes, M. A. "Anxiety in the Gifted: Pluses Minuses." *Roeper Review,* 6:2 (1983), p. 70.

Hardy, G. *The Canadian Charter of Rights and Freedoms: A Guide for Students. A Teacher's Manual.* The People's Law School, 1984/85.

Thompson, D. C. "Charter of Rights Leading to a Maze of Silliness?" *The Globe and Mail*, Toronto, June 13, 1985.

48

Student Activities

Poetry Appreciation I

> **Purpose:** • **To assist the student in clarifying his or her values**
> • **To encourage thoughts about citizenship and survival**

The following poems are from 'It's Not Always a Game/Un Eté d'illusions (All About Us, Box 7000, Ottawa, Ontario, 1973)

Remembrance Day, Nov. 8, 1973

When my Grandma died
we cleaned out her old house
we cleaned out desks and drawers
found old papers and letters
stamps still upon them
we burned most of them
in an old rusted barrel
on a windy November day

In burning these things
we destroyed many
memories of the past.
One we did not destroy
was addressed to my great-grandmother,
It said,
Dear Mrs. Ripley,
  I know you have already had a letter
from the Regt. about the death of your
son Robert . . .
  I know what it is like to lose a son,
but you have been asked to bear more
than your share of this war in the
loss of two brave sons . . .
  I might add that if I can I shall
KEEP Vincent for you.

Robert Donaldson.

— *Elizabeth Baldridge,*
Grade 6.

Words

Living, they say, takes courage today,
But in Parliament
A man is only as good as his speeches.
The talks go on,
But so do wars.
A poem is written,
A life is lost.
Words don't mean a thing.

Sharon Westerby,
Grade 4.

Vietnam

In Vietnam the buildings rise,
Up to the dark blue creamy skies,
Where trees grow tall
And also green,
Except in the battlefields
Where bullets gleam,
To find their marks
In people's hearts,
Where all pride dies.

John Pratt,
Grade 5,
Calgary, Alberta

I think war is sorrow and cruelness for freedom. My uncle is in the army
and told me.

Shelly Nemeth,
Grade 3,
Calgary, Alberta.

Why

Why did somebody invent guns?
Why do Mother and Father get divorced?
Why do people die?
Why do people kill?
Why do people hate each other?

Carl De Luca,
Grade 3,
Vancouver, British Columbia.

When I think of war I think of the soldiers and how they suffered through it. I feel like throwing up sometimes. I also know that the soldiers didn't like it. I know all this because I saw it on T.V.

Heike Heinke,
Grade 3,
Calgary, Alberta.

Probe Questions

1. Why are wars fought? Think beyond the obvious reasons.
2. What are your feelings about war?
3. What is heroism?
4. Have you talked to people who have fought in wars? What were their feelings about war? What were their feelings on heroism? Complete an oral history or research project on this topic.
5. What are viable alternatives to war? Is there a better way? Think of reasons listed or cited for question one. What alternatives are there to war as a means of "settling differences"?

Who Cares?

Who cares if the world's in a frenzy?
Who cares if we're always at war?
We are happy here
In our little suburbs, locked out from all the problems.
We don't have a care in the world!
There is no poverty, no starvation
Nothing to fret about.
We are smart now.
Caring for our little families
Hassling over our little problems.
The outside world is someone else's trouble.
No need for us to worry about that;
We have our own life to live.
We can't be bothered with our difficulties.
What could we do anyway?

Kathy Burrows,
Age 13,
Point Claire, Quebec.
It's Not Always a Game, *p. 173.*

Discussion Questions

1. Define "apathy."
2. Why does apathy sometimes cause problems? How might involvement create difficulties? Elaborate on responses. Give personal examples which clarify your response to each question.
3. Is Kathy serious or cynical when she says, "The outside world is someone else's trouble?" Give reasons for your response.
4. Where might the "What could we do anyway?" response lead?
5. In what ways might active involvement ensure a "voice"?
6. Why does involvement relieve one's conscience?
7. How does Kathy's poem make one feel?
8. Write a poem about caring and involvement.

*　　　　　*　　　　　*

The Age

I bowed my head to pray
But the words were trapped
Somewhere between the heart and the soul.
Alone here in the temple of perfection
Isolated from a world gone fetid
Barely breathing, suffocated by contradiction
As if we were crazy jigsaw pieces
In a puzzle with no solution.

Technological advances pave the way for devolution
While amidst crusty capitalism, there lurks a revolution
The spoken word echoes errantly
The hypnotic screen blips incessantly
Global villages burn
Prophets are spurned
At home, leaders plead the fifth amendment
And broken commandments herald the age of individuality

Alone I weep
As the temple becomes a cave
Outside the animals rage
And so soon I behave
As if I were one.

Allan Hardy,
Elementary Teacher,
Metro Separate School Board, Toronto.

Future Shock

Hung up on words
Put down by faces
Shouting, but never heard
Trapped in endless races.
So here we wait in one of life's stations
Hoping that our train comes in
Gravy trains and milk trains
Gathering speed, but patience is a fragile thing
And sometimes a fist clenches so tight
That everything is crushed
And what was once a good life
Is now merely dust

Bells peel and echo
Trapped forever in a noiseless sky
Leaders ignite the inferno
Young children cry.
Alone we stand on life's final mountain
Hoping to be caressed by the divine hand
Commands and reprimands
It seems that most people never change
Never living with the end in mind
And when skies finally darken
I hope we don't find
That we've all been forgotten.

Allan Hardy

Probe Questions

1. Having carefully read the two poems, write down one word that best captures your immediate feeling.
2. Using the above answer, identify one image from each of the poems and use them to explain your feeling.
3. Is there a valid reason for the poet's despair? Explain your answer by referring to your perceptions of the world.
4. "Ignorance is Bliss." Do you agree or disagree with this statement as it is specifically related to nuclear arms? You may express your answer in poetic form.
5. Imagine you are the hero in the film, "War Games," and you are trying to convince the NORAD officials of their folly. Which poem would you choose to explain yourself and why?

Poetry Appreciation II

Purpose:	• To further the personal development of each child
	• To encourage respect for individualism

The Sun and the Moon

The sun is filled with shining light
It blazes far and wide
The moon reflects the sunlight back
But has no light inside.

I think I'd rather be the sun
That shines so bold and bright
Than be the moon, that only glows
With someone else's light.

Elaine Laron,
from Free to Be You and Me, *ed. Thomas*
(New York: McGraw-Hill, 1974). Reprinted by
permission of Free To Be Foundation, New York.

Probe Questions

1. What natural phenomena is Elaine using to express her feelings?
2. Why does Elaine choose to be the sun?
3. Do you shine yourself or reflect someone else's light? Would you like to change? Note details about your change or transformation.
4. Is it important to shine yourself? Why?/Why not?

Write your own poem about the sun, the moon, the planets, galaxies. Can you express your feelings through metaphors?

Research

Find out about humanitarian people who were concerned with human rights and who did much to promote equality and egalitarian standards of living.

Consider how standing up for rights or principles allowed these people to help many other people. Why is this an important aspect of individualism?

Probe Questions

Define and discuss interdependence.

Does interdependence begin in the home or the classroom? Why?

Devise rules for living interdependently in the classroom.

*   *   *

The Game

A game with no winner
A game with no end
Where everyone loses
And no one can mend

The sadness, the sorrow
Which the game left behind.

Laura Giegerich, Grade 6,
from Girls Will Be Women, ed. B. Nickerson, 1975.

Probe Questions

1. To what game is Laura referring? Think beyond the obvious. Interpret the poem on different levels.
2. Have you played games where no one won? Describe a game where there is no winner. Why do you enjoy/dislike this type of game?

*   *   *

Nuclear Bomb

The bare,
deserted,
strip of land
was dry
and rocky.
As I walked
along,
I felt like
a nuclear bomb
had just hit.
The road
seemed
to go on
for ever
and ever . . .

Markham Breitbach, Grade 5,
Orangeville, Ontario.

1. How can we avoid destructive "games"? If it isn't possible to avoid the games, humans sometimes attempt to "win" or preserve supremacy at any cost? Why is this attitude a reasonable/unreasonable one?

Clarification: If opponents are using aggressive tactics, of any type, do we find ourselves in a situation where we have to use the same type of tactics? Explain your response using personal and global terms.

*   *   *

Reality

42 is reality.
No!
I dress
Therefore
I am.
Or maybe,
I think
Therefore
I am.
No!
That can't be
Right.
My reality
Is what
I make of it
People are what
I believe them
To be.
No!
They are what
They believe
Themselves
To Be.
Better yet,

We each have a
Reality
Peculiar to
Ourselves.
It is as
Good
As we make it.
Hey you!
Yes, you!
Jump over Here
and
Join
Me
In my
Reality.
No!
It is
Our
Reality
We
Love,
Therefore
We
ARE.

Kate Armstrong, Grade 9,
Orangeville, Ontario

Probe Questions

1. Are there different perceptions of reality? Explain.
2. How can varying perceptions of reality have direct effects on our actions?
3. What conclusions about reality does the poet express in her poem?
4. How might the poet's view of life affect her actions?
5. Is it fair and appropriate to judge others by our view of reality? Give reasons for your response.
6. To what degree are we responsible for our destinies?

Universal Human Rights

> **Purpose:** • To assist children in identifying rights and analysing issues
> • To encourage good citizenship

Where, after all, do universal human rights begin? In small places, close to home—so close and so small that they cannot be seen on any map of the world. Yet they are the world of the individual person; the neighborhood he lives in; the school or college he attends; the factory, farm, or office where he works. Such are the places where every man, woman, and child seeks equal justice, equal opportunity, equal dignity without discrimination. Unless these rights have meaning there, they have little meaning anywhere. Without concerted citizen action to uphold them close to home, we shall look in vain for progress in the larger world.

Eleanor Roosevelt at the United Nations,
March 1958.

Probe Questions

1. In your opinion, where do universal human rights begin? Explain what you mean.
2. Do you agree with Mrs. Roosevelt's statement that human rights on a global basis will have little significance unless we work as good citizens to uphold them at home? Explain your ideas.
3. List and discuss some rights you have as an individual. List and discuss some rights you have as a child. List and discuss some rights you have as a Canadian citizen. Compare your rights with those of other children throughout the world.

Note to Teacher:
This discussion might lead to follow-up studies using newspaper articles, magazine articles, chapters from books and encyclopedias. Research reports, projects, interest talks, and guest speakers could follow initial discussion and ensuing research.

Preamble to the Charter of the United Nations

WE THE PEOPLES OF THE UNITED NATIONS DETERMINED

   TO SAVE succeeding generations from the scourge of war, which twice in our lifetime has brought untold sorrow to mankind, and
   TO REAFFIRM faith in fundamental human rights, in the dignity and

the worth of the human person, the equal rights of men and women and of nations large and small, and

TO ESTABLISH conditions under which justice and respect for the obligations arising from treaties and other sources of international law can be maintained, and

TO PROMOTE social progress and better standards of life in larger freedom,

AND FOR THESE ENDS

TO PRACTICE tolerance and live together in peace with one another as good neighbors, and

TO UNITE our strength to maintain international peace and security, and

TO ENSURE, by the acceptance of principles and the institution of methods, that armed force shall not be used, save in the common interest, and

TO EMPLOY international machinery for the promotion of the economic and social advancement of all peoples,

HAVE RESOLVED TO COMBINE OUR EFFORTS TO ACCOMPLISH THESE AIMS.

Quoted from L. Goodrich, E. Hambro, and A. Simons, *Charter of the United Nations: Commentary and Documents.* 3rd and rev. ed. (New York: Columbia University Press, 1969), p. 19.

Ideas and Reflections on Human Rights

> Purpose: • **To encourage a responsible attitude, good citizenship, and the ability to adhere to principles**

Explore the following issues through discussion and reading. Write ideas on chart paper. Display ideas on bulletin board. Add to ideas throughout the year. Use first-hand information, reading, and research.

Issues and Topics

1. Discuss human rights and responsibilities. Define each.
2. Rights of the individual. Why does the group have to be considered when considering individual rights? Are individual and group rights equally important? Give reasons.

3. Discuss class rights and responsibilities. Brainstorm for ideas. List and vote on acceptance of ideas.

4. Rights of Humans. Read and discuss the "Preamble to the Charter of the United Nations."

5. (a) How do the rights of children differ from those of adults? Since both are individuals, is the difference just?

   (b) According to some people, children can be hurt by the difference. At what times can this happen?

   (c) Read about the movements which attempt to give children more rights in legal areas. Do you believe they are necessary? Give reasons for your response.

   (d) Study the rights of children at various stages throughout history. Comment on your discoveries. React to information. Share information with others. Prepare an interest talk on one aspect of your information.

6. Discuss Eleanor Roosevelt's statement that universal human rights begin in small places close to home, and that until the rights of the individual person are met, universal human rights will have little meaning anywhere.

   Include examples from current events in your discussion.

7. (a) With all rights comes responsibility. How do we learn to accept the responsibility that comes with rights? What happens when people fail to accept the responsibility that is given with rights? (Examples include disobeying rules, laws, or exploiting power.)

   (b) Think about rights which you have been denied because of irresponsible behavior.

   (c) Find out about countries which have progressed or regressed according to their handling of power and acceptance of responsibility. Comment. Be specific. How can we help others be responsible (i) in the class? (ii) in the neighborhood? and (iii) in the world?

Consumerism

> **Purpose:** • To assist children to understand their needs and values
> • To help children develop a responsible attitude concerning consumerism

U. K. Teenage Girls on Spending Spree

LONDON — If Britain is on the skids, no one has told the country's three million teenage girls who blow an estimated $2-billion a year on clothes, records, and other tokens of the easy life.

Girls between 12 and 18 spend some $89-million a year on cosmetics and toiletries, $91-million on confectionery and $1-million on blue jeans alone, according to a new survey based on interviews with 1,500 girls done by a large magazine publishing company.

"We were absolutely staggered by some of the results," William McIntosh, advertising manager of magazines for young people at Pic Magazines Ltd., said. "We knew teenage girls were big spenders, but not on this scale."

The girls also pick up their parents' habits. Almost one third of those between 16 and 18 smoke cigarettes and one quarter of these smoke more than a pack a day. Half the smokers wish they could give it up.

More than 40 percent of the 18-year-old girls visit pubs regularly.

Less surprisingly, 98 percent of teenage girls have a record or tape player and more than 70 percent own both. In all, they buy more than 20 million records and three million tapes a year.

The average pocket money for a 12-year-old girl is about $1.87 a week and the average net income of 18-year-olds working full time is $45 a week.

Money may not come as quickly as it can in North America, but the girls, like so many in Britain today, seem willing to work long hours to acquire the trappings of the good life.

Ian Rodger, The Globe and Mail, *Toronto, Saturday, August 27, 1977. Reprinted by permission of The Globe and Mail, Toronto.*

Probe Questions

1. What does this article indicate about the values of teenage girls in the United Kingdom?
2. In your opinion, how would these values compare to those of teenagers in Canada?

3. How important is it to clarify your values in pre-adolescent years?
4. What makes values clarification difficult for teenagers?
5. Why do some people find it difficult to make and maintain a decision which conflicts with the choices or values of their friends or acquaintances?
6. When are people able to defend and adhere to their decision(s)? What feelings sometimes result from adherence to beliefs or choices?
7. When do you pay a price for individuality?
8. Is individuality worth the price you pay? Why?/Why not?

Suggested Readings

Biehler, Robert F. *Psychology Applied to Teaching.* 2nd ed. Boston: Houghton Mifflin, 1974.

Constitution of Canada: Final Report of the Special Joint Committee of the Senate and the House of Commons. Ottawa, 1979

"Declaration on the Rights of the Child". United Nations General Assembly, November 20, 1959.

Dobler, Lavia. *Arrow Book of the United Nations.* New York: Scholastic, 1970.

Graves, Charles. *Eleanor Roosevelt.* New York: Yearling Books, 1968.

Hart, Carole; Pogrebin, Letty; Rodgers, Mary; and Thomas, Marlo. *Free to Be You and Me.* New York: McGraw-Hill, 1974.

Phenix, Philip H. *Realms of Meaning.* New York: McGraw-Hill, 1964.

Schaef, Anne W. *Women's Reality.* Minneapolis, MN.: Winston Press, 1981.

Soward, F., and McInnis, E. *Canada and the United Nations.* Westport, CT.: Greenwood, 1975.

Teaching Human Rights. United Nations, 1963.

"Walking Small — Kids Have Rights Too!" says Jacob Two-Two. "Kids Have Rights Too." *Weekend Magazine*, November 6, 1976.

"Where Have All the Children Gone?" *Nous Journal* (Spring/Summer, 1977).

4

Senior/Youth Interaction

Introduction

"As research shows only too clearly, we have all been subjected to negative images about age and aging. Yet age is inevitable. With more and more of us living longer and longer, these negative images need to be dispelled and countered." (Grambs, 1980)

Labels usually suffer from inadequacies because they are relative to the ever-changing societal context. The appropriateness of the label, "senior citizen," for those sixty-five years or older today may soon include those fifty to sixty-five years old. Nevertheless, the term is used here in the conventional sense to represent those citizens now retired and living the last one-third to one-half of their life span. Indeed, as life expectancy, especially for females, moves in the direction of one hundred years plus (projected that 100,000 persons in the United States will be over one hundred years old by the year 2000), we are talking about fifty years plus of formal retirement!

In another fifty years, about 20 percent of North America's population will be over sixty-five years old. In Canada, there will be two retired persons for every one eighteen-year-old. In another fourteen years, 14 percent of Canada's total population (about twenty-eight million) will be over sixty-five. This is based on a 1.4 child-per-family birth rate and an intake of fifty thousand immigrants per year. The implications of this aging factor for health care, pensions, and the economy are now major issues. Governments are worried about the monetary resources that will be needed to support the increase in the number of senior citizens during a time when the general economy is in heavy deficit and less income is generated for benefits to the elderly.

Several projects have been initiated in various schools in order to facilitate awareness of and communication between the younger and older generations. These "intergenerational" school activities frequently result in supportive relationships between the young student needing affection and tutoring and the senior citizen needing to be wanted and helpful. It is a form of the "extended family" which has virtually disappeared in much of North America except in certain strong ethnic households where the deep-rooted tradition is preserved.

At the same time, working against those positive efforts are two current and significant sources of bias against aging. Much of children's popular literature (Towler, 1983) and the television medium exalts the youth cult and the male gender. Older persons are usually depicted as flat, lifeless, dull, or uninteresting male figures. While it is granted that much of the market is aimed at the youth, the combined effect fosters the attitude that the elderly are insignificant or worthless.

Another related and poorly treated concept is that of death. In the same children's popular literature and television, the concept appears infrequently and is treated in an unemotional and insensitive fashion.

These findings suggest that more opportunities need to be made available to students to nurture positive attitudes and relationships among the young and old. Since the gifted are usually more at ease in conversing with adults and more desirous of helping others well in advance of their nongifted peers, they may be highly susceptible to activities that promote and engage them in that direction.

One example of such a sensitizing activity would be an assignment to create a *TV Viewing Log* consisting of a centre box for the name of a television character, real person, or individual in a commercial. This box is then surrounded by six other boxes with the following questions posed for the student to respond in each box:

1. Describe person (physically and personality).
2. Is the person an important part of the program's plot?
3. What products are older people associated with in commercials?
4. How is the person treated by other characters/individuals?
5. Does the TV portrayal of the person seem real to you? Is the person portrayed positively or negatively?
6. If you were older, would you like to be like this person? Why?/Why not?

> "Typically, they (the gifted) experience more special and emotional pressures from everyday living with their gifts. The interaction of these non-intellective factors with extraordinary cognitive abilities determines the extent to which highly gifted children are able to realize their intellectual, productive, and creative potential."
>
> (Brown, 1984).

References

British Broadcasting System. "December Flower". A TV drama about a middle-aged widow seeking the companionship of her sick, elderly aunt. BBC, 1985.

Brown, M. M. "The Needs and Potential of the Highly Gifted: Toward a Model of Responsiveness." *Roeper Review*, 6:3 (February 1984), pp. 123-7.

Grambs, Jean D. "Grow Old Along with Me . . . Teaching Adolescents about Age." *Social Education* (November/December 1980).

Ministry for Senior Citizens Affairs. *Guide for Senior Citizens: Services and Programs in Ontario.* Toronto, Ont.: Queen's Park.

Prime Time School Television. *Thinking about Aging.* Chicago, Ill: PTST, 40 E. Huron, 60611, 1982.

Secretariate for Social Development. *The Elderly in Ontario: An Agenda for the '80s.* Toronto, Ont: Ontario Government Bookstore, December 1981.

Seniors Secretariat. *Elderly Residents in Ontario: An Overview.* A summary of 14 papers on characteristics of 900 Ontario seniors. Toronto, Ont.: Publications Services, Ontario Government Bookstore, 1985.

Towler, John O. A. *A Comparison of the Concepts of the Aged as Reflected in Canadian Children's Popular Literature and Television Programs.* SSHRCC Research Project. Waterloo, Ont.: Renison College, University of Waterloo, October 1983.

Student Activities

The following extracts can be used as discussion starters or extended activities based on this theme.

Reflections on "Old Age"

1. "It is the world's pity," cried [Prince] Siddartha [before becoming Buddha], "that weak and ignorant beings, drunk with the vanity of youth, do not behold old age! Let us hurry back to the palace. What is the use of pleasures and delights since I myself am the future dwelling-place of old age."

   Buddha recognized his own fate in the person of a very aged man, because, being born to save humanity, he chose to take upon himself the entirety of the human state. In this he differed from the rest of mankind, for they evade those aspects of it that distress them. And above all they evade old age.

   — Simone De Beauvoir, The Coming of Age
   (New York: G. P. Putnam's Sons, 1972), p. 1.
   Reprinted by permission of The Putnam Publishing Group from
   Coming of Age *by Simone De Beauvoir.*
   English translation copyright © 1972 by Andre Deutsch,
   Weidenfeld and Nicholson and G. P. Putnam's Sons.
   Reproduced by permission of Andre Deutsch Ltd., London.

2. "The Council's concern, according to the brief, stems from its basic goal of trying to help create a province in which it is possible to grow old with dignity and a sense of usefulness, to have a choice of one's own destiny and where people have concern for each other and rejection is no longer acceptable. The choice of when to work and when to retire should be left in the individual's hand."

   Especially for Seniors
   (Winter '76-'77)

3. In every area of the world, including the most economically and cultural-ly advanced, there are many people whose psychological needs are not satisfied, who are unable to give and receive love and who have no feeling of worth either of themselves or others.

   — William Glasser, Reality Therapy *(New York:*
   Harper & Row, 1965), p. 9.

4. The purified image of themselves that society offers the aged is that of the white-haired and venerable sage, rich in experience, planning high above the common state of mankind; if they vary from this, then they fall below it. The counterpart of the first image is that of the old fool in his dotage, a laughing-stock for children. In any case, either by their virtue or by their degradation they stand outside humanity. The world, therefore, need feel no scruple in refusing them the minimum of support which is considered necessary for living like a human being.

— *Simone De Beauvoir,* The Coming of Age, *p. 4.*
Reprinted by permission of The Putnam Publishing Group from
Coming of Age *by Simone De Beauvoir.*
English translation copyright © 1972 by Andre Deutsch,
Weidenfeld and Nicholson and G. P. Putnam's Sons.
Reproduced by permission of Andre Deutsch Ltd., London.

The Little Old Lady

That little grey-haired lady
Is as old as old can be.
Yet once she was a little girl
A little girl like me.

She liked to skip instead of walk
She wore her hair in curls
She went to school at nine and played
With other little girls.

I wonder if, in years and years
Some little girl at play
Who's very like what I am now
Will stop to look my way.

And think: "That grey-haired lady
Is as old as old can be
Yet once she was a little girl
A little girl like me."

Rodney Bennett
(source unknown)

Poetry Appreciation

Purpose: • **To develop a responsible and caring attitude**
• **To encourage involvement and good citizen-ship**

Teacher reads the words of the song "Hello in There". Inform students that the song was written by John Prine and recorded by Joan Baez on her album "Diamonds and Rust" (A & M Records of Canada Ltd.). Further state that the words of the song will be read silently and that the Baez recording of the song will be played.

Teachers may wish to tell students that Prine and Baez are both American folk singers who were well known in both Canada and the United States in the late '60s — a time of optimism and undaunted concern over human rights. Many of the songs written by Prine and Baez urge people to strive for compassion and to play fairly in the game of human inter-action and politics.

Ask students to think carefully about the words of "Hello in There" and to decide whether or not the song has a serious message. Remind students to recall and compare some of the statements made by their friends during the Senior/Youth Exchange.

Discussion should then follow the reading and listening session.

Probe Questions

1. What is the theme of the song?
2. The aging of humans is compared with the aging of certain elements in nature. What are the differences?
3. What does Prine suggest we do for the elderly?
4. Is this request one that is difficult to fulfil? Is it unreasonable? Discuss.
5. Why do many people fail to help the aged in the manner Prine suggests? Are the reasons valid?
6. Where are the children of this elderly couple?
7. In reference to "Davey," Prine again criticizes society. What is he say-ing? Is the criticism warranted? Explain.
8. Did you enjoy the poem? Why?/Why not?
9. Did it give more relevance to some of the statements made by your friends during the Senior/Youth exchange? Specify.

*   *   *

Senior Citizens
Newspapers in Education

Bremerton, Wash. (AP) — A sixth-grade girl who wrote to President Carter about her "very special" grandpa has managed to get a resolution introduced in Congress pushing for creation of a National Grandparents' Day.

Anne Tillery, 11, wrote to the President in February, suggesting a grandpa's day.

"My grandpa is Mr. Barney Tillery and he is very special. He tries to help everybody and that is why I would like to have a grandpa's day for him and all grandpas," she wrote.

She added, "Maybe we should start thinking about a special grandma's day, too. But we'll work on that later."

A presidential assistant replied to Anne, explaining that although Carter supported her idea, he could make such a proclamation only when authorized by Congress.

So Anne wrote her congressman, Representative Norm Dicks (Dem. Wash.) and he introduced a slightly modified version of her suggestion in the House of Representatives on Monday.

Reprinted by permission of The Canadian Press, Toronto.

Probe Questions

1. Do you think a special day should be set aside for grandparents? Give reasons for your answer.
2. Did the Grade 6 girl who wrote to President Carter about "her very special" grandparent voice the opinion of many children? Base your answer on your own experiences. You might wish to conduct a survey in your class or school to find out how many children would like to have a special day set aside for grandparents.
3. Do you agree with Anne Tillery in her belief that we should first have a grandpa's day and later start thinking about a grandma's day? What practical alternative might you suggest?
4. How did Anne find out about the workings of government?
5. If she had known more about official procedure might she have acted differently? In what way?
6. What is your reaction to Anne's actions and her voicing of her opinion?
7. How and when do you voice your opinion?

Seniors Visit School

> **Purpose:** • To assist the student in learning to respect and communicate with people of another generation
> • To promote the development of a responsible and caring attitude toward seniors
> • To encourage intergenerational involvement

The teacher will arrange for the senior citizens a separate and special presentation of a play, operetta, choir, or gymnastics performance. Posters will be made and placed in various Senior Citizens' buildings to advertise the event. One class will be responsible for baking cookies, cakes, and breads to be served at a tea which will follow the performance. The baking will be done at home by the children. A committee of four students will delegate responsibilities for baking, arranging, and serving the food. Volunteer parents will prepare tea and coffee for the occasion.

Children should dress in a manner which will show that they respect the decorum expected by many elderly people. Also, like adults, children tend to behave in a manner analagous to that which their dress symbolizes.

Related Activities

1. Recipes used by children in preparation for the tea party may be brought to school, where they will be compiled in a recipe book. Both metric and imperial measures will appear in the book which will later be given to or exchanged with a senior citizen.
2. The recipe used by the children for the tea party may become an insertion in a gift booklet made up of the children's stories, poems, drawings, and so on.

A Celebration of History

Purpose: • **To encourage interaction between seniors and youth**
• **To give students some insights into local history through the eyes of those who have experienced it**

Directions

Involve students in oral history for a study project using the framework provided by the Basic Inquiry Model and the Renzulli Triad Model of enrichment.

One of the criticisms often levelled at the teaching of history is its reliance on secondary sources, particularly textual materials. For the gifted child, such traditional presentations do not accommodate their full interests or abilities. This underemployment of effective resources is heightened by the over-reliance on the socratic method of instruction. With the deployment of an activity-oriented and problem-solving approach to history this subject can come to life for the gifted learner.

A variety of approaches to teaching and learning styles will actively involve and excite the gifted learner. For example, techniques of interviewing, simulations, the use of audio-visual equipment, and first-hand interactions are some of the effective and affective means used to report, design, and create a final product.

One of the best resources available in this approach is the local community and, more specifically, its senior citizens. The exchange of ideas fostered through this interchange between generations can be useful in creating mutual respect. More importantly, it allows a fulfilment of needs for both young and old.

*   *   *

Sample Unit
Glimpses of Dufferin County
Faces of Dufferin

To celebrate Dufferin County's Centennial Year, a number of activities were explored by students in the Intermediate withdrawal classes for the gifted.

Students began by exploring activities using *THE BASIC INQUIRY MODEL* (1978). Initial experiences included guest lecturers from the Historical Society, the book *Into the High County* (1975), and relevant newspaper articles. Once the general question "In what ways might Dufferin County's Centennial year be actively celebrated?" was formulated, the group began the process of selected products which would best express their interests. The following items composed this list of intended products:

1. A videotape in which local senior citizens would reminisce about the development of Dufferin County, with specific reference to education and to their roles in such advancement.
2. A calendar which would capture the flavor of the local landscape and accommodate the students with artistic inclinations.
3. A story book which, although similar in content to the videotape, would best accommodate the prosaic-minded student.

Students and resource teacher projected and presented a budget for the project to the Board officials. The project was approved.

The Renzulli Triad Model of Enrichment was employed in order to provide a framework and differentiate activities.

Exploration of exposure activities which appealed to the entire group included brainstorming, browsing, topical speakers, and relevant field trips. The training exercises, so important in product preparation, were more specific and group-oriented. Those preparing the prose and photo booklet *Faces of Dufferin*, and the videotape "Glimpses of Dufferin," were given much training in research and interviewing skills, as well as in the skills necessary for portrait photography.

The groups working on the videotape were individually trained in the multi-faceted use of audio-visual equipment and the general preparation of a television program.

The products of this local history study were favorably received. The ninety-minute videotape "Glimpses of Dufferin" was circulated amongst the schools in Dufferin County and was aired as a special Centennial celebration program on local cable networks. For this product the assistance of a retired professional photographer and television producer and director proved invaluable. Local cable studios made their professional facilities and some staff (that is, cameraman) available.

The booklet *Faces of Dufferin,* a series of interviews with some elderly local residents, was prepared by transcribing a selected group of audio-taped interviews. Originally these tapes had been prepared to screen potential videotape subjects and to give students an opportunity to hone their interviewing skills. In order to supplement the booklet presentation, photographs, prepared by trained students, were taken and printed. Techniques in characterization, specifically the ability to transfer the essence of the verbal interview into print, were directed by the resource teacher. Like the selection of the videotape subjects, the written interviews which best captured the subjects' uniqueness were published in the final product, *Faces of Dufferin.*

The third intended product, a calendar depicting local scenes, never reached its ultimate goal because of prohibitive costs. The quality of the individual sketches indicated that the students benefited from their sessions with local artists.

Student feedback indicated that this unique approach to history was both enjoyable and meaningful, especially the insights gained through exposure to local history as seen through the perceptions of senior citizens of Dufferin County.

Interviewing Seniors

> **Purpose:** • To assist the student in the collection of historical data from primary sources
> • To develop the ability to make decisions

Interview senior citizens to gather data for an oral history review and to compare their life-style as children to students' present life-style.

Students should be given training in interviewing skills and then prepare to interview a senior citizen in the community. The student should display poise, confidence, respect, and empathy throughout the interview, and should be able to ask supplementary questions to make questions explicit or to hitch-hike on responses which provide starting points for further discussion.

Students will have gained experience from interviews with peers, parents, teachers, as well as from simulated interviews with characters from books, prominent Canadians, and famous people. Students should take turns playing the role of interviewer and interviewee.

Questions should be checked by the teacher who will offer suggestions or constructive criticism if necessary. Students may use a cassette tape recorder for the final interview and videotape the final interview.

Related Activity

Have resource books available so that students may read interesting stories on the lives of people now classified as senior citizens.

Visiting Seniors

> **Purpose:** • To help the student develop a responsible attitude through involvement and caring for others
> • To help students and seniors find "significant others" in their lives

During the spring term students in the class will make five or six weekly visits to a senior's residence.

Students and senior citizens will each fulfill two basic psychological needs:

(1)   the need to be loved — through involvement and friendship;
(2)   the need to feel worthwhile to ourselves and others.

The student will gain respect for others and thus enhance self-respect. The student will develop a responsible, empathic, and humanistic attitude towards elderly people. It is my opinion that this humanistic attitude must be fostered in a society which frequently ignores or rejects those who are perceived as having ceased to be functional. Senior citizens will view youth in a light other than the negative perspective occasionally presented by the media.

The student obtains information through interviewing, listening to others, and discussion.

The student becomes involved and interested in community affairs and people of another generation.

Possible group activities should be discussed with the class and individual activities listed as follows:

    I.   Group: (a)   oral reading
               (b)   dramatics
               (c)   poetry recitation
               (d)   crafts
               (e)   interviews
               (f)   square dancing
               (g)   discussion
               (h)   sharing experiences through photos, slides, interest talks

    II.   Individual: In a private interview each student relates what he or she expects to share with the senior citizen and what he or she expects to learn from the senior citizen.

After the teacher has outlined individual objectives for each student in the class, a liaison from the senior citizens' home will work with the teacher to match each child with a senior citizen. The socialization tea may facilitate the matching process. Following the tea at the senior citizens' home or the school performance and tea, certain children may request to be matched with specific senior citizens. Their wishes should be respected and fulfilled if possible.

Example of Individual Objectives

Amy McNab — Ottawa, Ont., Grade 6

(a) The student is prepared to share the following activities with the senior citizen:
    (i)   flower-making — paper and cloth
    (ii) reading aloud
    (iii) discussions on past, present, and future
    (iv) weaving
    (v) read essays and stories (written this year) to senior citizen and ask for constructive criticism and evaluation.

(b) The student wants to learn the following from the senior citizen:
    (i)   past history; experiences; problems; secrets as a child

(ii)   cooking — recipes
(iii) pets — talk about them.

Alex Hay — Ottawa, Ont., Grade 6

(a) The student is prepared to share the following activities:
   (i)   reading aloud — discussion on books
   (ii)   sharing experiences through discussion
   (iii) talking and questioning about the past
   (iv)   interest in medicine

(b) The student wants to learn the following from the senior citizen:
   (i)   past history
   (ii)   crafts — decoupage
   (iii) photos and slides — world travels
          (Alex has lived in South Africa, Scotland, Botswana, England,
          Europe, Canada, Mexico. He was born in South Africa.)

Emily Lye — Ottawa, Ont., Grade 6

(a) The student wants to share the following activities:
   (i)   art — drawing — critical evaluation from senior citizen
   (ii)   reading aloud — animal stories
   (iii) discussion on humane treatment to animals
   (iv)   general discussion

(b) The student wants to learn the following from the senior citizen:
   (i)   reading aloud: exchange of stories
   (ii)   crafts, art
   (iii) discussion on topical issues
   (iv)   share photo viewing and discussion ◆

Related Activities

Read aloud and discuss with class A. Philippa Pearce's *Tom's Midnight
Garden* (1958). The book tells of the affinity and interaction between a
young boy and an elderly lady, first through dreams and the unconscious
and finally through reality.

*   *   *

Evaluation

> **Purpose:** • **To evaluate the youth/senior citizen exchange**
> • **To provide constructive criticism which will
>   help teachers design their own program**

Following the senior citizens' visitation, a questionnaire was sent to
students and senior citizens. Responses were received from approximate-

ly half the students and senior citizens. The following is a compilation of questions and directly quoted responses which reveal the worth of the program. Modifications will be made in next year's program from the observations and responses.

Student Questionnaire and Responses

Question: 1. What particular aspects did you enjoy about your visits to the senior citizens' home?

Responses:
a. I liked her and enjoyed visiting her every week.
b. Her stories about her life.
c. She lived where I live and explained how it was.
d. She was fun and she was ready when we arrived.
e. What I learned about history and crafts.
f. I also met her friends. They were very kind.
g. Being with a person older than myself and accepting his differences.
h. Hearing about their experiences when they were children.
i. Having lunch at her house.
j. Looking at pictures with her.
k. Reading to her.
l. They looked forward to all our visits.
m. I liked being able to share my thoughts with her.
n. There was a lot of recreation which I thought was good.
o. We went up to their apartments for private talk.
p. Things we did were fun.
q. We were welcomed with open arms.
r. We learned that when she was younger she worked for a hockey manufacturing company.

Question: 2. What were your disappointments, if any? (Note: Answers should be explicit and honest.)

Responses:
a. No disappointments at all.
b. The visits were too short.
c. People asked questions about us being in the building.
d. I found that sometimes there was a silence and nobody could say anything.

Question: 3. What did you learn from this experience? Explain. Was it worthwhile?

Responses:
a. It was worthwhile because it was fun.
b. It let me recognize myself and share my ideas. I learned about the "good old days."

c. I learned about their background and enjoyed it
    very much. I think the program was very worth-
    while for me and I hope for my senior citizen.
d. I made a friend.
e. I learned that cities and towns were different in
    his generation. I saw what it was like before.
f. I learned that I can relate to older people.
g. I learned that senior citizens enjoy having young
    people with whom they may discuss ideas and
    thoughts.
h. I learned that people at that age weren't really
    disabled, but very active.
i. They were very kind.
j. I learned how people fifty years ago lived and I
    also learned that senior citizens are a lot more
    than just "old people."
k. Yes, I think it was worthwhile because I became
    more aware of how people feel about children.

Question: 4. Aside from your friend, did the people in the
                     building give you a warm reception?

Responses: a. Yes, because I knew most of them from being with
                     my grandmother.
                 b. Yes, I enjoyed it, they were very nice to us.
                 c. They gave me a warm welcome and I thank them
                     for it.
                 d. Yes. I think they were happy to see children.
                 e. Yes. They showed us around the building.
                 f. They were polite to me when I asked a question.
                 g. Sometimes we took the stairs and other people in
                     the building would complain to us.
                 h. Yes. I think people were very warm because they
                     accepted us.

Question: 5. Do you have suggestions for future exchanges
                     with senior citizens?

Responses: a. Get outside more when the weather is nice and
                     have a picnic or something fun.
                 b. Give us more time together.
                 c. This year's visitations, I thought, were perfect.
                     The only thing I regret was not having more time
                     with them to talk and do arts and crafts.
                 d. Yes. I request that it be a bit longer and maybe
                     not so many people for one senior citizen.
                 e. The end of the day would be more suitable so you
                     would not have to worry about time.
                 f. Do it exactly the same as before.

Question:	6.	Did your image of the elderly change as a result of the exchange? Specify.
Responses:	a.	Yes, before I did not know it was so much fun with them.
	b.	My image of the elderly did not really change because I have a grandmother of my own.
	c.	Yes. I found that they were a lot friendlier and smarter than I thought they were.
	d.	Yes. They are a lot kinder than I imagined.
	e.	It sure did! I didn't bother much with senior citizens before, but now I realize they too are people.
	f.	Not very much. They seemed to be much more involved in current events than I had thought.

Senior Citizen Questionnaire and Responses

Question:	1.	What, in particular, did you enjoy about the student visits to your apartment?
Responses:	a.	Very good students.
	b.	General knowledge of world events. They seemed to enjoy school work very much. Very interested in handicrafts, especially sewing, which I do myself.
	c.	They are so relaxed and ready to cooperate in answering questions about their future. They enjoyed the visits.
	d.	The student who visited me was a pleasure to be with.
	e.	He displayed a very polite and friendly attitude. It was nice finding out about our similar interests (stamps, etc.).
	f.	The boy was very bright and interested in photography and brought slides for me to see. He told me about his family. Each time we had cookies and juice. He enjoyed this very much.
	g.	His kind, smiling personality. His above-average intelligence. His interest in gaining knowledge concerning senior citizens.
	h.	The ease with which the children conversed. The interest which they expressed in local affairs. Their joy in living and the pleasure they showed in the contacts with older people. Their joy in sharing.

Question:	2.	Did you find the exchange was sometimes tiring? Yes *1*, No *11*, No response *1*. If yes, please tell us why?
Responses:	a.	I found three students too many, although I was very fond of all of them.
	b.	I did not find the exchange tiring, but was at a loss to know how to converse with the children. After running out of conversation, we played a game.
Question:	3.	The visits were Wednesday, April 27; Friday, May 6; Thursday, May 19; Friday, May 27; Friday, June 10. Would you have preferred fewer visits? Comments: Yes *3*, No *8*, With qualification *1*, Non-committed *1*.
Responses:	a.	The weekly visits seemed appropriate.
	b.	No, but I found the June visit a little late.
	c.	Unfortunately, I had to miss three of the visits.
	d.	I would have preferred the visits once a month.
	e	Same number.
	f.	Every second week.
	g.	I think four visits would be sufficient.
	h.	I think once a month over a longer period of time.
Question:	4.	How did you feel about the length of the visit? Was it too long — too short? *5* Comments: No response *7*.
Responses:	a.	About right. (Added by senior citizens.)
Question:	5.	How many students would you prefer to receive each visit? Indicate by tick.
Responses:	a.	Number of Students: Two *9*, Three *2*, Four *1*, Five *1*.
Question:	6.	Did your image of the students change as a result of the exchange?
Responses:	a.	Yes. Contrary to news reports of school teaching systems which are being criticized, I found them very knowledgeable for Grade 6 students.
	b.	Very surprised at what they knew.
	c.	I found them very informed.
	d.	Yes. I found my girls were very intelligent and considerate. I was interested in what they did in school today compared to when I went.
	e.	Being a mother, grandmother, and now great-grandmother, my image of students has always been good.

f.   Having a young grand-daughter about the same age, I found my visitor most interesting and bright.

g.   They seemed more friendly and we got to know each other.

h.   No, I would not generalize on the image I hold of students any more than any other group. I'm sure there are many excellent students and perhaps some not so good. I must add that the two children who visited me were really well-behaved.

i.   No. We had very many exchanges of ideas and they were very interested and replied with their own ideas.

j.   In a way, I was amazed at the knowledge the girls had and compared this with what I recall at the same age.

k.   Very much. Even though there are a few bad kids I found there are a great many really fine boys and girls. Polite, kind, and interesting.

Question: 7.   Did you receive any undesirable feedback from other residents during these visits? No *13*. Comments or qualifications.

Qualifications:

Responses: a.   They took the stairs instead of the elevator. I told them to use the elevator.

b.   Everyone was quite pleased to have the students.

c.   Some said they couldn't be bothered having them.

Question: 8.   Do you have any suggestions for future student exchanges of this nature?

Responses: a.   Because we are older we like to rest in the afternoon. I would prefer visits in the morning.

b.   We should keep plans flexible.

c.   No. Although I feel this could be a great idea for some people, I don't feel it is for me.

d.   Possibly if we were together as a group (such as a picnic outdoors), we would get better acquainted.

Additional Comments

These visits helped the students better understand the elderly. By the same token, elders gain by mingling with young people. In each case, views and ideas are stimulated, while popular myths and misconceptions are eradicated.

Oral Comments Made by Students During Weekly Visits to Seniors' Residences

1. "We are getting to know the senior citizen. My senior citizen is becoming a friend."
2. "We learn about the past."
3. "My grandparents live in Vancouver and I don't see them often. This seems like visiting them."
4. "We compared prices of things when my senior citizen was a child and now. Were things ever cheap. I'd like to live in that time period — but only for a week."
5. "I think we will show more consideration towards all older people now."
6. "My friend said that when we visit, she feels young again."
7. "My senior citizen said that all her children and grandchildren live in Toronto and she seldom sees them. That is why she is so happy when we visit."

Future Directions

a. Incorporate this program with other similar social agency programs.
b. Plan a picnic.
c. Begin and end visits earlier in school year.
d. Involve two students with each senior citizen.
e. Work optimistically towards continued and reciprocal enjoyment, involvement, and commitment.
f. Have senior citizens (especially former teachers) come to the classroom as volunteers. They could help children with writing, reading, crafts, and so on. For example, one senior citizen — who had been a teacher and a renowned local artist — spent several days working with gifted children on pen and ink sketches of buildings of historical or architectural significance.
g. Invite senior citizens to accompany children on field trips to explain historical aspects of certain areas or changes in architecture. Excellent history lessons may be taught in this manner.

Suggested Readings

Curriculum Ideas for Teachers. *Research Study Skills: History and Geography,* Intermediate Division. Toronto: Ministry of Education, 1979.

De Beauvoir, Simone. *The Coming of Age.* New York: G. P. Putnam's Sons, 1972.

Glasser, William. *Reality Therapy.* New York: Harper & Row, 1965.

Laurence, Margaret. *The Stone Angel.* Toronto: McClelland and Stewart, 1968.

Paier, Robert. *The Pied Piper.* New York: McGraw Hill, 1979.

Pearce, A. Philippa. *Tom's Midnight Garden.* New York: Oxford University Press, 1970.

Pogue, Betsy. *Interview Research.* East Aurora, N.Y.: DOK, 1983.

Renzulli, Joseph. *The Enrichment Triad Model.* Connecticut: Creative Learning Press, Inc., 1977.

Shakespeare, William. *King Lear.* New York: Longmans, 1964.

Towler, John O. *A Comparison of the Concepts of the Aged as Reflected in Canadian Children's Popular Literature and Television Programmes.* University of Waterloo, 1983, 5 SHRC grant 492-80-0026. This research indicates the presence of discriminating stereotyping (sexism and ageism) in both "popular" children's literature and select television programs. Numerous factors combine to foster the image of insignificant and worthless elders.

Especially for Seniors. Toronto: The Ontario Advisory Council on Senior Citizens.

Films
1. The Shopping Bag Lady (Learning Corporation of America. Released in Canada by Marlin Motion Pictures.)
2. The Lillith Summer (Canadian Learning Company, 2229 Kingston Road, Suite 203, Scarborough, Ontario, M1N 1T8.)
3. The Fall of Freddie the Leaf (Canadian Learning Company, 2229 Kingston Road, Suite 203, Scarborough, Ontario, M1N 1T8.)

5

Literary Extensions

Introduction

> Literature, we said, is conscious mythology; it creates an autonomous world that gives us an imaginative perspective on the actual one.
>
> N. Frye, *The Bush Garden, Essays on the Canadian Imagination,* p. 151.

During the past few years a number of studies have been directed toward the differences between the gifted student and the average learner. The result of such efforts is that educators in this field are now able to compile character profiles of the gifted student comprehensively.

The following section of the book attempts to elucidate upon one particular trait: the heightened awareness and perception revealed by the gifted child toward moral ethical issues. The gifted child's aptitude for problem solving has proven invaluable in such an exercise. Aside from aptitude, the gifted child also enjoys and is stimulated by the endless possibilities that often arise during a values oriented activity. Such open-ended exercises as outlined in this chapter are specifically designed to enhance the moral and social development of the bright child.

This approach is in line with developmental theories, for example, Maslow and Kohlberg, and current curricular programs such as the "Ethical Inquiry" component of the Philosophy for Children materials.

The process inherent in such tasks or activities encourage gifted children to look beyond the superficial and extract meanings and patterns that often remain undetected. Such critical and creative thinking abilities may be nurtured through discussion and dramatic modes, which are encouraged in this unit.

The quest for satisfying experiences is often a life-consuming task. Such a journey may no doubt be furthered and directed toward positive discoveries by employing the concept of vicarious learning. Literature, particularly the books recommended in this chapter, is an excellent means of facilitating the gifted child's search for meaning and self-actualization. For the gifted child who experiences difficulty in relating to others or finding intellectual peers, the world of literature can be a rich and varied resource. Bibliotherapy, which is used as an aid to self-understanding, is an underused teaching and learning strategy. It is a positive experience to be able to identify with the heroine in *Anne of Green Gables*, a girl who is not only bright and articulate, but is also capable of activating and controlling her environment. For children who have found their uniqueness to be a mixed blessing, Charles Wallace in *A Wrinkle in Time* provides an interesting role model. Although he possesses an extensive vocabulary, Charles uses it selectively as those around him are threatened by his big words. However, when he chooses to remain silent, the situation becomes worse since Charles is perceived as being slow to understand. Such a situation could produce anxiety and isolation. However, Charles, with the help of a supportive family, is able to use his unique gifts to solve problems and restore harmony within his environment.

A Bridge to Terabithea is somewhat similar in that it provides an example of two bright children releasing themselves from frustration, boredom, and misunderstanding by creating an imaginary world.

As a final example, *The Mixed Up Files of Mrs. Basil E. Frankweiler* presents Claudia and Jamie coping admirably in the world of ideas, budgets, planning, and problem solving. Identifying with these children can help the gifted appreciate their uniqueness and harness the magic of their minds. In its most effective form this then is the interest of literary extensions.

Book(s) of the Month Program

> **Purpose:**
> - **To encourage avid reading and critical thinking**
> - **To further the personal development of each child**

The following list of carefully selected novels is given to each student in September. It serves as a "recommended reading" list. Most of these books should be available in the classroom library, school library, and public library. The books have been selected to include such topics as identity crises, moral dilemmas, family and societal interrelationships. Also selected are books which delineate reversals in stereotyped male–female roles.

Monthly Selections

Ten books are chosen from the reading list and titles are displayed on a chart. Each child is asked to (1) read one of the suggested books, and (2) be prepared to discuss it in an oral conference or book interview, or submit a written book report, or (3) complete a creative product based on some aspect(s) of the book.

One or two of the books should be discussed with students who have read them. In other instances, students are encouraged to discuss their choices with peers. Discussions should focus on controversial statements in the book, identify issues which concern the main characters, moral or ethical decisions the characters attempt to resolve, and a critical evaluation of the book. The discussion of important themes such as friendship, freedom, war, maturation, self-actualization, acceptance of responsibility, good and evil forces, and so on, should help the student gain new insights into the world of reality and solve problems in his/her environment. Sample discussion questions on *The Little Prince, Tom's Midnight Garden,* and *The Wizard of Earthsea* are included.

*   *   *

Recommended Reading List Used in Discussion of Values*

"If language is the clothing of life, no child should go naked into the world."
— Dan Fader.

Adams, Richard.
　　Watership Down, 1972; New York: Macmillan, 1974.

---

*Where possible, dates are included to fit books into historical perspective.

Adamson, Joy.
> *Born Free.* New York: Random House, 1960.
> *Forever Free.* New York: Random House, 1962.

Alcott, Louisa May.
> *Little Women,* 1868; New York: Penguin Books, 1983.
> *Little Men,* 1871; New York: Penguin Books, 1984.
> *Jo's Boys,* 1886; New York: Penguin Books, 1984.

Anderson, Hans Christian.
> *Fairy Tales,* 1830.

Atwater, Richard and Florence.
> *Mr. Popper's Penguins.* Boston: Little, Brown & Co., 1938.

Baker, Rachel.
> *The First Woman Doctor,* 1944.

Barrie, Sir James.
> *Peter Pan.* London: Hodder, 1944.

Baum, L. Frank.
> *The Wonderful Wizard of Oz,* 1900; Mineola, N.Y.: Dover Publications, 1972.
> *The Marvellous Land of Oz,* 1904; New York: Penguin Books, 1985.
> *Dorothy and The Wizard in Oz,* 1908; Mineola, N.Y.: Dover Publications, 1984.
> *The Road to Oz,* 1909; New York: Ballantine, 1984.
> *The Magic of Oz,* 1919; New York: Ballantine, 1981.

Bentley, Phyllis.
> *The Young Brontes.* Folcroft, PA.: Folcroft Library Editions, 1960.

Beresford, Elisabeth.
> *The Wombles,* 1968.

Berton, Pierre & Patsy.
> *The Secret World of OG.* Toronto: McClelland & Stewart, 1961.

Blume, Judy.
> *Are You There God, It's Me, Margaret.* New York: Bradbury Press, 1970.
> *Deenie.* New York: Bradbury Press, 1973.
> *Tales of a Fourth Grade Nothing,* 1972; New York: Dell Publishing Co., 1981.
> *Then Again Maybe I Won't.* New York: Bradbury Press, 1971.

Blyton, Enid.
> *The Mountains of Adventure.* London: Macmillan, 1949.

Bond, Michael.
> *A Bear Called Paddington:* London: Collins, 1958.

Burnett, Frances Hodgson.
> *A Little Princess.* Cutchogue, N.Y.: Buccaneer Books, 1981.

The Secret Garden, 1911; New York: Dell Publishing Co.,
1971.

Burnford, Sheila.
The Incredible Journey. Boston, MA.: Little, Brown & Co.,
1961.

Byars, Betsy.
The Summer of the Swans. New York: Viking-Penguin, Inc.,
1970.

Callaghan, Morley.
Luke Baldwin's Vow, 1948; Richmond Hill, Ont.: Scholastic-
TAB, 1975.

Cameron, Eleanor.
A Room Made of Windows. Boston: Little, Brown & Co., 1971.

Carr, Emily.
Klee Wyck, 1941; Richmond Hill, Ont.: Irwin Publishing Co.,
1966.
The Book of the Small, 1942; Richmond Hill, Ont.: Irwin
Publishing Co., 1966.
Growing Pains, 1946; Richmond Hill, Ont.: Irwin Publishing
Co., 1966.

Carr, M. J.
Young Mac of Fort Vancouver, 1940.

Carroll, Lewis.
Alice's Adventures in Wonderland, 1864; New York: Bantam
Books, 1981.
Through the Looking Glass, 1871; New York: Macmillan, 1963.

Clark, Ann Nolan.
Secret of the Andes. New York: Viking-Penguin, Inc., 1952.

Clarke, Pauline.
The Twelve and The Genii, 1962.

Cleary, Beverly.
Henry Huggins. New York: Morrow, Williams & Co., Inc.,
1950.

Clemens, Samuel.
The Adventures of Tom Sawyer, 1871; New York: Dodd, Mead
& Co., 1984.
The Adventures of Huckleberry Finn, 1884; New York: Norton,
1977.

Conford, Ellen.
Dreams of Victory. Boston: Little, Brown & Co., 1973.

Cook, Lyn.
The Bells of Finland Street, 1966.

Corbett, Scott.
The Hockey Girls. New York: E. P. Dutton, 1976.

Corrivenu, Monique.
    A Perfect Day for Kites. Toronto: Groundwood, 1981.

Dahl, Roald.
    James and The Giant Peach. New York: Alfred A. Knopf,
    1961.

Davidson, Margaret.
    Helen Keller's Teacher, 1965; New York: Scholastic Inc., 1972.

De Angeli, Marguerite.
    Door in The Wall, 1949; New York: Scholastic Inc., 1984.

Defoe, Daniel.
    Robinson Crusoe, 1791; Richmond Hill, Ont.: Scholastic-TAB.

Dickens, Charles.
    A Christmas Carol, 1843; New York: Holiday House, Inc.,
    1983.

Dickens, Monica.
    Summer at World's End. London: Heinemann, 1971.

Dodge, Mary M.
    Hans Brinker, 1865; New York: Penguin Books, Inc., 1985.

Doyle, Arthur Conan.
    The Tales of Sherlock Holmes, 1892; *The Adventures of
    Sherlock Holmes.* New York: Penguin, 1981.

Duncan, Frances.
    Cariboo Runaway, Don Mills, Ont.: Burns and MacEachern,
    1976.
    Kap-Sung Farris. Don Mills, Ont.: Burns and MacEachern,
    1976.

Eager, Edward.
    Half Magic. San Diego, Ca.: Harcourt Brace Jovanovich, Inc.,
    1954.
    Knight's Castle, 1956; San Diego, Ca.: Harcourt Brace
    Jovanovich, Inc., 1985.

Epstein, Sam & Beryl.
    George Washington Carver. Easton, MD.: Garrard Publishing
    Co., 1960.

Estes, Eleanor.
    The Moffats, 1941; San Diego, Ca.: Harcourt Brace Jovanovich,
    Inc., 1968.

Falkner, J. Meade.
    Moonfleet, 1898; Salem, NH.: Merrimack Pub. Circle, 1984.

Farjeon, Eleanor.
    The Little Bookroom, 1956; Boston: David R. Godine, Inc., 1984.

Farley, Walter.
    The Black Stallion. New York: Random House, Inc., 1941.

Fisher, Dorothy Canfield.
    Understood Betsy, 1917; New York: Avon Books, 1973.

Fitzgerald, John D.
    The Great Brain. New York: Dial Books for Young Readers, 1967.
    More Adventures of the Great Brain. New York: Dial Books for Young Readers, 1969.
    The Great Brain at the Academy. New York: Dial Books for Young Readers, 1972.

Fitzhugh, Louise.
    Harriet The Spy. New York: Harper & Row Junior Books, 1964.
    Nobody's Family Is Going to Change. New York: Farrar, Strauss & Giroux, Inc., 1974.

Fleming, Ian.
    Chitty, Chitty, Bang, Bang. Mattituck, N.Y.: Amereon Ltd., 1964.

Fynn.
    Mister God This Is Anna, 1974; New York: Ballantine, 1985.

Forbes, Esther.
    Johnny Tremain. Boston: Houghton Mifflin Co., 1943.

Freeman, Bill.
    Shantymen of Cache Lake. Toronto: James Lorimer & Co., 1975.
    Last Voyage of the Scotian. Toronto: James Lorimer & Co., 1976.
    First Spring on the Grand Banks. Toronto: James Lorimer & Co., 1978.
    Harbour Thieves. Toronto: James Lorimer & Co., 1984.

Gates, Doris.
    Blue Willow. New York: Viking-Penguin, Inc., 1940.

German, Tony.
    Tom Penny. Toronto: McClelland and Stewart, 1977.

Gipson, Fred.
    Old Yeller. New York: Harper & Row Publishers, Inc., 1957.

Grahame, Kenneth.
    The Wind in the Willows, 1908; New York: Bantam Books, Inc., 1982.

Graves, Charles.
    Eleanor Roosevelt. Easton, MD.: Garrard Pub. Co., 1966.

Green, Roger.
    King Arthur and His Knights of the Round Table, 1953; New York: Penguin Books Inc., 1974.

Greene, Constance.
  A Girl Called Al. New York: Viking-Penguin, Inc., 1969.
  Your Old Pal, Al. New York: Dell Publishing Co., 1979.

Haar, Joapter.
  Boris, 1966; New York: Delacorte, 1970.

Hemon, Louis.
  Maria Chapdelaine. Salem, NH.: Ayer Co. Pub. Inc., 1921.

Henry, Marguerite.
  Born to Trot. Chicago, Ill.: Rand McNally, 1950.
  King of the Wind. Chicago, Ill.: Rand McNally, 1948.

Hewitt, Marsha and Mackay, Claire.
  One Proud Summer. Toronto: The Women's Press, 1981.

Hickcook, Lorena A.
  The Story of Helen Keller, 1958; New York: Putnam
  Publishing Co., 1974.

Hill, Kay.
  Glooscap and His Magic. Toronto: McClelland and Stewart,
  1963.

Holling, Holling C.
  Paddle-to-the-Sea. Boston: Houghton Mifflin, 1941.

Houston, James.
  Black Diamonds. New York: Atheneum, 1982.
  Frozen Fire. New York: Atheneum, 1977.

Hughes, Monica.
  Keeper of the Isis Light. New York: Atheneum, 1981.
  The Guardian of Isis. New York: Atheneum, 1982.
  The Isis Peddlar. New York: Atheneum, 1983.
  The Tomorrow City, 1978.
  Crisis on Conshelf Ten, 1975.

Hunt, Irene.
  Across Five Aprils, 1965; New York: Ace Books, 1984.

Irving, Washington.
  Rip Van Winkle, and the Legend of Sleepy Hollow, 1819; New
  York: Smith Pubs., 1980.

Jemison, Mary.
  Indian Captive, 1941.

Killilea, Marie.
  Karen, 1952; New York: Dell Publishing Co., 1983.

Kipling, Rudyard.
  The Jungle Books, 1895; Mattituck, N.Y.: Amereon Ltd., 1976.
  Just So Stories, 1912; Mattituck, N.Y.: Amereon Ltd., 1976.

Kjelgaard, Jim.
  Big Red, 1945; New York: Bantam Books Inc., 1976.

Outlaw Red, 1953; New York: Bantam Books Inc., 1977.

Knight, Eric.
Lassie Come Home, 1940; New York: Dell Publishing Co., 1975.

Konigsburg, E. L.
From the Mixed-Up Files of Mrs. Basil E. Frankweiler. New York: Atheneum, 1967.
Jennifer, Hecate, Macbeth, William McKinley and Me, Elizabeth. New York: Atheneum, 1967.
Throwing Shadows. New York: Atheneum, 1979.

Korman, Gordon.
Bugs Potter. New York: Scholastic Inc., 1980.
Beware of the Fish. New York: Scholastic Inc., 1979.
Go, Jump in the Pool. New York: Scholastic Inc., 1979.
The War with Mr. Wizzle. New York: Scholastic Inc., 1982.
This Can't Be Happening at McDonald Hall. New York: Scholastic Inc., 1979.

Kurelek, William.
A Prairie Boy's Winter. Boston: Houghton Mifflin, 1973.
A Prairie Boy's Summer. Boston: Houghton Mifflin, 1975.

Lang, Andrew.
The Blue Fairy Book. Magnolia, MA.: Peter Smith Pub. Inc., 1889.

Lawson, Robert.
Ben & Me, 1939; New York: Dell Publishing Co., 1973.
Rabbit Hill, 1944; New York: Penguin Books, Inc., 1977.

L'Engle, Madeleine.
A Wrinkle in Time, 1963; New York: Dell Publishing Co., 1976.
A Wind in the Door. New York: Dell Publishing Co., 1974.
Camilla, 1965; New York: Delacorte Press, 1981.
Dragons in the Waters, 1976; New York: Dell Publishing Co., 1982.

Le Guin, Ursula. The Earthsea Trilogy:
A Wizard of Earthsea. Boston: Houghton Mifflin, 1968.
The Tombs of Atuan. New York: Atheneum, 1971.
The Farthest Shore. New York: Atheneum, 1972.

Le Roy, Gen.
Emma's Dilemma, 1975.

Lewis, Elizabeth.
Young Fu of the Upper Yangtze, 1932; New York: Holt, Rinehart and Winston, 1973.

Lewis, C. S.
The Chronicles of Narnia (1950-56); New York: Macmillan, 1983:

The Lion, The Witch and The Wardrobe (1970).
Prince Caspian (1969).
The Voyage of the Dawn Treader (1969).
The Silver Chair (1967).
The Horse and His Boy (1969).
The Magician's Nephew (1970).
The Last Battle (1970).

Lindgren, Astrid.
Pippi Longstocking. New York: Penguin Books, 1977.
Pippi in the South Seas. New York: Viking-Penguin, Inc., 1959.

Little, Jean.
Kate. New York: Harper and Row Junior Books, 1971.
From Anna. New York: Harper and Row Junior Books, 1972.

Lofting, Hugh.
The Story of Doctor Doolittle, 1920; New York: Lipp Junior Books, 1980

London, Jack.
The Call of the Wild, 1903; New York: Macmillan, 1970.

Lorenzini, C.
The Adventures of Pinocchio, 1880; Chicago: Rand McNally, 1982.

Lunn, Janet.
Twin Spell. New York: Penguin Books, Inc., 1968.

Magnussen, Karen.
Karen: The Karen Magnussen Story, 1973.

Major, Kevin.
Far From Shore. New York: Dell Publishing Co., 1983.

McKenzie, Ruth.
Laura Secord. Toronto: McClelland and Stewart, 1971.

Montgomery, L. M.
Anne of Green Gables, 1908; New York: Bantam Books, Inc., 1976.
Anne of Avonlea, 1909; New York: Bantam Books, Inc., 1979.
Anne of the Island, 1915; New York: Bantam Books, Inc., 1976.

Morey, Walter.
Gentle Ben. New York: E. P. Dutton, 1965.

Mowat, Farley.
Lost in the Barrens. New York: Little, Brown & Co., Inc., 1956.
The Dog Who Wouldn't Be, 1957; New York: Bantam Books, Inc., 1981.
Owls in the Family, 1961; New York: Bantam Books, Inc., 1981.

The Black Joke. Toronto: McClelland and Stewart, 1962.

The Curse of the Viking Grave. New York: Little, Brown & Co., Inc., 1966.

Nesbitt, E.

The Story of The Treasure Seekers.

The Would-Be-Goods, 1901.

Five Children and It, 1902, New York: Dell Publishing Co., 1986.

The Phoenix & The Carpet, 1904; New York: Penguin Books, Inc., 1985.

The Railway Children, 1906; New York: Penguin Books, Inc., 1959.

The Story of the Amulet, 1906; New York: Penguin Books, Inc., 1959.

Nichols, Ruth.

The Marrow of The World. New York: Atheneum, 1972.

North, Sterling.

Rascal, 1963; New York; Avon Books, 1976.

Norton, Mary.

The Borrowers, 1952; New York: Harcourt, Brace, Jovanovich, 1965.

The Borrowers Afield. New York: Harcourt, Brace, Jovanovich, 1955.

The Borrowers Afloat. New York: Harcourt, Brace, Jovanovich, 1961.

O'Brien, Robert C.

Mrs. Frisby and the Rats of NIMH. New York: Atheneum, 1971.

O'Dell, Scott.

Island of the Blue Dolphins. Boston: Houghton Mifflin, 1960.

O'Hara, Mary.

My Friend Flicka, 1967. New York: Dell Publishing Co., 1976.

Paperny, Myra.

The Wooden People. Boston: Little, Brown & Co., 1976.

Patterson, Lillie.

Martin Luther King Jr., Man of Peace. Easton, MD.: Garrard Publishing Co., 1969.

Pearce, A. Philippa.

A Dog So Small, 1962.

Minnow on the Say, 1955.

Tom's Midnight Garden, 1970; New York: Dell Publishing Co., 1986.

Porter, Eleanor.

Pollyanna, 1927; Larrels, N.Y.: Lightyear Press, Inc., 1976.

Ransome, Arthur.
    Secret Water, 1939; Salem, NH.: Merrimack Pub., 1980.
    Swallows & Amazons, 1930; Salem, NH.: Merrimack Pub.,
    1981.
    Swallowdale, 1931; Salem, NH.: Merrimack Pub., 1980.
    Peter Duck, 1933; Salem, NH.: Merrimack Pub., 1980.
    We Didn't Mean to Go to Sea, 1937; Salem NH.: Merrimack
    Pub., 1983.
    Coot Club, 1937; Salem, NH.: Merrimack Pub., 1980.

Richler, Mordecai.
    Jacob Two-Two Meets the Hooded Fang. New York: Bantam
    Books, Inc., 1975.

Roberts, Charles.
    Red Fox, 1905; Boston: Houghton Mifflin, 1972.

Saint-Exupéry, Antoine de
    The Little Prince, 1943; San Diego, Ca.: Harcourt Brace
    Jovanovich, 1982.

Saunders, Marshall.
    Beautiful Joe, 1934; Toronto: McClelland and Stewart, 1972.

Scott, Sir Walter.
    Ivanhoe, 1819; New York: Airmont, 1964.

Selden, George.
    The Cricket in Times Square. New York: Farrar, Straus &
    Giroux, 1960.

Seredy, Kate.
    The Good Master. New York: Dell Publishing Company, 1963.

Sewell, Anna.
    Black Beauty. New York: Ace Books, 1949.

Sidney, Margaret.
    Five Little Peppers and How They Grew, 1948. 3rd ed. New
    York: Lothrop, Lee & Shepard Books, 1976.

Silverberg, Robert.
    Time of the Great Freeze, 1964.

Smucker, Barbara.
    Days of Terror. Scottdale, PA.: Herald Press, 1979.
    Underground to Canada. Scottdale, PA.: Herald Press, 1977.

Sperry, Armstrong.
    Call It Courage, 1940; New York: Macmillan, 1971.

Spyri, Johanna.
    Heidi, 1884; New York: Penguin Books, Inc., 1983
    Heidi Grows Up, 1940.
    Heidi's Children, 1950.

Sterling, Dorothy.
    Freedom Train. New York: Norton, 1954.

Stevenson, R. L.
> *Treasure Island,* 1883; New York: Bantam Books, 1981.

Stowe, Harriet Beecher.
> *Uncle Tom's Cabin,* 1929; New York: Bantam Books, 1981.

Streatfield, Noel.
> *The Painted Garden,* 1949; New York: Dell Publishing Co., 1984.

Sutcliffe, Rosemary.
> *The Eagle of the Ninth.* Oxford: OUP, 1954.
> *The Lantern Bearers.* Oxford: OUP, 1959.
> *Knight's Fee.* Oxford: OUP, 1960.

Swift, Jonathan.
> *Gulliver's Travels,* 1726. (Voyages I & II)

Tolkien, John R. R.
> *The Hobbit,* 1938; Boston: Houghton Mifflin, 1984.
> *The Lord of the Rings,* 1954; Boston: Houghton Mifflin, 1974.

Travers, Pamela L.
> *Mary Poppins,* 1934; San Diego, CA.: Harcourt, Brace, Jovanovich, 1981.

Verne, Jules.
> *Around the World in Eighty Days.* New York: Dell Publishing Co., 1964.

Wahl, Jan.
> *The Furious Flycycle,* 1968.

White, E. G.
> *Stuart Little.* New York: Harper & Row Junior, 1945.
> *Charlotte's Web.* New York: Harper and Row Junior, 1952.
> *The Trumpet of the Swan.* New York: Harper & Row Junior, 1973.

White, T. H.
> *The Sword in the Stone.* New York: Dell Publishing Co., 1938.
> *The Once and Future King,* 1958; New York: Berkley Pub., 1983.

Wilder, Laura I.
> *The Little House in the Big Woods,* 1932; New York: Harper & Row Junior, 1953.
> *By the Shores of Silver Lake,* 1939; New York: Harper & Row Junior, 1953.
> *The Long Winter,* 1940; New York: Harper & Row Junior, 1953.
> *Little Town on the Prairies,* 1941; New York: Harper & Row Junior, 1953.
> *These Happy Golden Years,* 1943; New York: Harper & Row Junior, 1953.

Wiggin, Kate D.
    Rebecca of Sunnybrook Farm, 1903; New York: Dell
    Publishing Co., 1986.

Wilde, Oscar.
    The Happy Prince, 1888; Morristown, N.J.: Silver Burdett Co.,
    1985.

Wilson, Eric.
    The Ghost of Lunenburg Manor. Don Mills, Ont.: General
    Publishing, 1982.
    The Lost Treasure of Casa Loma. Don Mills, Ont.: General
    Publishing, 1982.

Wyndham, Lee.
    The Lady with the Lamp. Easton, MD.: Garrard Pub. Co.,
    1969.

Wyss, Johann David.
    Swiss Family Robinson, 1813; New York: Dell Publishing Co.,
    1960.

A Sample Discussion Lesson

Purpose: • **To encourage critical reading and thinking**
• **To promote respect and understanding of others**

A. Tom's Midnight Garden — A. Philippa Pearce

1. p. 1: "If, standing alone on the back doorstep Tom allowed himself to weep tears, they were tears of anger. He looked his goodbye at the garden and raged that he had to leave it . . ."

   (a) Have you ever been forced to leave something you loved? If so, how did you react? If not, how do you think you would react?

   (b) The author tries to leave some question as to whether or not Tom actually cries. Do you think boys should be as free to cry or to openly express emotion as girls are? Give reasons for your response.

2. p. 3: "Tom closed the car window and sat back in his seat, in hostile silence. His uncle cleared his throat and said: 'Well, I hope we get on reasonably well.' This was not a question, so Tom did not answer it. He knew he was being rude, but he made excuses for himself. He did not much like Uncle Alan, and he did not want to like him at all, and Aunt Gwen, she's worse, because she's a child lover, and she's kind."

   (a) How would you rate Tom's behavior? Is it excusable? Why?/Why not?

   (b) How would you react under similar circumstances?

3. Despite the disapproval of adults in their environment, Tom and Hatty carve initials on yew trees, climb sun-dial walls, and play with bows and arrows.

   (a) Are they being intentionally disobedient? Wrong? Playful? Why?

   (b) What would you do in their garden under similar circumstances?

B. A Wizard of Earthsea — Ursula LeGuin

1. p. 29: ". . . he hungered to learn, to gain power. . . . Ged crouched among the dripping bushes wet and sullen, and wondered what was the good of having power if you were too wise to use it, and wished he had gone as prentice to that old weatherworker of the Vale . . ."

(a) Of what fault will Ged have to rid himself before he may become a true wizard?

(b) Do adults lose the imaginative powers they had as children? If so, why might this be true? Do you think the narrator is a typical adult?

C. The Little Prince — Antoine de Saint-Exupéry

1. p. 17: "Grown-ups love figures. When you tell them you have made a new friend, they never ask you any of the questions about essential matters. They never say to you, 'What does his voice sound like? What game does he love best? Does he collect butterflies?' Instead, they demand: 'How old is he?' "

(a) Have you found these habits to be characteristic of adults? If so, do you agree with their overriding concern with figures? Why?/Why not?

(b) What other factors, aside from those mentioned by the narrator, could give adults some information on your new friend?

2. p. 18: "To forget a friend is sad. Not everyone has a. friend."

(a) Does the narrator value friendship? Explain.

(b) Express your ideas about friendship.

Book Report Format

> **Purpose:** • **To develop critical reading**
> • **To present a format which provides a more comprehensive study of values in the novel**

1. *Basic Information:*
   (a) Name of Book (title underlined)
   (b) Author
   (c) Classification (fantasy, biography, autobiography, historical fiction, science fiction)
   (d) Number of Pages
   (e) Publisher
   (f) Illustrator
2. What is the *setting* of the story (time and place)?
3. (a) From whose *point of view* is the story written?
   (b) How does the narration (that is, first person, third person . . .) affect the story?
4. *Characters:*
   (a) Name the central character.
   (b) Describe one central character:
      (i) physical description
      (ii) "inner feelings" — attitudes, morals, ideas.
      (iii) mention an identity crisis, if applicable.
5. *Plot:*
   (a) Purpose
   (b) One setback or problem (describe in fifty words or less).
   (c) Briefly outline one *moral or ethical dilemma* faced by a character. Show how this dilemma and its resolution furthers plot and/or character development.
   (d) Triumph or Resolution of Problem
      (i) good and evil forces in the novel
      (ii) parents of main character
         adults or authority figures in novel.
6. *Personal Evaluation of the Book:*
   (a) Write a short summary of your reaction to the book.
   (b) Note year in which book was written.
   (c) Paragraph of biographical information on the author.
   (d) Racist or sexist statements in novel (if applicable).

> Recognition of racist and sexist statements in the book should not undermine enjoyment and appreciation. It is important to find the year in which the book was written and appreciate the story in the proper historical context. *It is always important to read critically.*

*   *   *

Sample Responses

"Inner Feelings" — C. S. Lewis: The Lion, The Witch, and The Wardrobe
Lucy explores the professor's old mansion and discovers the magic wardrobe. She tries to convince Edmund, Peter, and Susan of her discovery but they refuse to believe her. Lucy is unable to enjoy any of the daily activities in which the children participate. Edmund continues to taunt Lucy but Peter and Susan feel very disturbed about the issue. They do not want to believe that their sister is telling lies.

Plot: Moral or Ethical Dilemma: — F. Mowat: Lost in the Barrens
Jamie and Awasin have to decide whether they should help Denikazi and the Chipeweyans in their attempt to hunt caribou on the Barrenlands. Awasin states that his Uncle Solomon doesn't think they should provide ammunition but his father "has never turned a hungry man away." Awasin chooses to follow his father's example.

The plot develops as Jamie and Awasin accompany The Chips on their quest. Jamie makes decisions without his uncle's presence or guidance and thus Jamie matures.

Identity Crisis: — L. Carroll: Alice in Wonderland
Example 1:
Alice addressed The Cheshire Cat, "Would you tell me please, which way I ought to go from here?"

"That depends a good deal on where you want to get to," said the Cat.
"I don't much care where ----" said Alice.
"Then it doesn't matter which way you go," said the Cat.

Example 2:
Alice replied, rather shyly, "I hardly know, sir, just at present — at least I knew who I was when I got up this morning, but I think I have been changed several times since then."

"What do you mean by that?" said the Caterpillar sternly. "Explain yourself!"
"I can't explain myself, I'm afraid, sir," said Alice, "because I'm not myself, you see."

*   *   *

The entire content of the novel may be interpreted as Alice's search for identity. She changes throughout the novel, and true to the nature of a dream, images of the self are revealed.

Alice is a poetic, verbal child whose mode of "survival" is through the spoken word. In this respect, she may be compared to Lucy Maud Montgomery's "Anne". Alice is also curious and persistent, thus she controls her environment and activates the situation in which she finds herself. In this manner and through self-questioning, she appears to come to terms with her identity.

Sample Book Reports

I Title: E. B. White: The Trumpet of the Swan

Basic Information: Fantasy; 210 pages; Harper and Row Publishers; Illustrator: Edward Prascino. Date: 1949.

Although Louis the swan was born in Canada, the setting of the story is generally in the United States in such places as Boston and Philadelphia. Most of the story takes place in Montana.

The story is written in the third person. Sometimes the author tells how the characters feel and sometimes he lets them give their point of view in their own words.

The major characters in the story are: Louis, the swan; Sam Beaver, the boy; Serena, a beautiful female swan; and Louis' mother and father.

When Louis, the swan, was born he was a grey colour, with an orange beak and orange legs. When he grew up he had white feathers and a black beak, and black legs. He was different from the other swans because he had no voice.

When Louis' father told him he had a speech defect, Louis felt scared and frightened. When he found out his father had stolen a trumpet, he felt guilty. He feels love for Serena, but unhappy because she spurns him for being different; he has an identity crisis when he feels he is different from other swans.

The purpose of the plot is to show how Louis managed to pay for the trumpet, and how he got over his voice problem and won Serena's love. Louis' one problem is that he came into the world lacking a voice. He couldn't communicate with his family and could not seem to attract the swan of his desire. In the story Louis comes across a moral problem when his father steals a trumpet so that Louis can be more like other swans. At first Louis feels happy about it, but then he feels he should pay for the trumpet. Louis gets different jobs to earn the money. He triumphs by finally winning the swan of his desire, and he solves his speech problem with his trumpet. Louis' father stole the trumpet so that his son could lead a reasonably normal life.

I like the way E. B. White made the animals able to talk to each other.

E. B. White was born in Mount Vernon, New York, in 1899. He wrote thirteen books of prose and poems. His two previous children's books, *Stuart Little* and *Charlotte's Web*, are modern classics for which he had been given the 1970 Laura Ingalls Wilder Award.

Kirsti Weeks,
Grade 7,
Ottawa, Ontario.

II Title: Arthur Ransome: We Didn't Mean to Go to Sea

Fiction, Puffin Books, 1969.

The characters are Jim Brading, and four children who are asked by Jim to spend a couple of days on his yacht, the Goblin. The children are John, who eventually wants to become a sailor; Rodger, who has many of the same ideas as his brother; Titty, who is very fond of animals; and Susan, who acts as mother of the four while they are on Jim's yacht. The setting for the novel is on board the Goblin, touring the harbours.

The four children find themselves at Alma Cottage, awaiting their father's return. The father had been to China on business and was to return by boat, entering at Harwich Harbour. Their stay had been quite boring until they met Jim Brading. Jim invited them to stay on his yacht for a couple of days. They would tour the various harbours, but he promised never to go out to sea. On the second day of their voyage, Jim anchored at low tide and rowed in to buy some petrol for the engine. He missed the bus and had to wait for the next one. Meanwhile, back at the yacht, the tide was rising. Suddenly the yacht started to drift and fog encircled them. John, Susan, Rodger and Titty were beginning to get worried. John didn't know quite what to do. The fog became thicker, making it very difficult to steer. Susan and Titty were beginning to get seasick. The boat rocked and jerked. It started to rain. They were out to sea. What would their mother say? It began to pour rain and the dark clouds blackened out the light. Susan and Titty were seasick. For the rest of the night John steered; Susan watched for buoys and logs; Titty and Rodger slept. Suddenly, a great mass of darkness loomed ahead. It was a steamer! The Goblin had no lights. How would they tell the steamer that they were straight ahead? Susan had an idea. She grabbed a bright red light. They were safe, but how would they make it through the night and back to Alma Cottage or Harwich Harbour again!

I liked this book very much. It is very exciting to read, because of all the adventures aboard ship. I recommend this book to anyone. It is both good reading and teaches you a lot about boats.

Sandy Connell,
Grade 6,
Ottawa, Ontario.

Creative Drama

Purpose: • **To provide an opportunity for personal reaction to ideas presented in print and for growth in decision making**

Divide students into small groups. Children are given time to prepare scenes for dramatization from novels they have read in this program. Teachers should use their own discretion as to the amount of time necessary for preparation. Some groups will use improvisation and will be ready within the period. Others will require time to write a script and to obtain costumes. Allow for individual differences as this is a creative exercise which calls upon many skills. It is appropriate to discuss the values inherent in the scenes.

Any of the ten examples given may be used for the first session. For follow-up lessons, children should be encouraged to choose their own scenes from books on the "recommended reading" list.

1. Lewis Carroll: *Alice in Wonderland.*
   Chapter VII — "A Mad Tea Party."
   Alice joins unusual guests in an interesting conversation at a mad tea party. The use of costumes and script adapted by the children can enrich this scene.

2. Frank Baum: *The Wizard of Oz.*
   Chapter II — "The Wonderful City of Oz."
   The great and terrible Oz listens and responds to the requests of Dorothy, The Scarecrow, The Tin Woodman, and the Cowardly Lion.

3. Myra Paperny: *The Wooden People*
   (a) Chapter VII — "Puppets in The Attic."
   Several children from the school come to watch Lisa, Teddy, Michael, and Suzanne put on a puppet show. Lisa instructs, ". . . follow the ushers up this ladder to the attic, I mean Mezzanine."

   (b) Chapter XI — "The Curtain Goes Up."
   As Papa ushers his "deceitful" children out of the auditorium, the judge announces that the Stein family and Tom, their partner, have won the grand prize for their magical puppet theatre.

4. Frances Duncan: *Cariboo Runaway.*
   Chapter 1 — "The Runaway."
   Elva explains to Tim that she is cutting her braids so that she will look more like a boy as she attempts to find her father in the goldfields.

5. Antoine de Saint-Exupery: *The Little Prince*.
   Chapter 2.
   The Little Prince gets the narrator to draw him a sheep. He is not satisfied until he receives a picture of a sheep in a box.

6. Frances H. Burnett: *The Secret Garden*.
   Chapter 14.

   Nole Streatfield: *The Painted Garden*.
   The Other Mr. B., Jane and Mr. Bryan J. Brown discuss the possibility of Jane playing Mary in *The Secret Garden*. They further discuss Mary's character as shown in the book and the film.

7. Farley Mowat: *Owls in The Family*.
   Chapters 2 & 3.
   Bruce, Billy, and Mr. Miller search for an owl's nest in bluffs on the prairie. They find a nest with three young owls in it. Mr. Miller suggests the owls are about the right age to take home for pets.

8. M. Richler: *Jacob Two-Two Meets The Hooded Fang*.
   Chapter 13.
   Jacob tells the Hooded Fang that he is not horrible, disgusting, mean, vicious, vile, or evil. The Hooded Fang denies these statements, but makes a deal with Jacob.

9. L. M. Montgomery: *Anne of Green Gables*.
   Chapter 16 — "Diana is Invited to Tea with Tragic Results."
   Diana Barry visits Anne for tea. Anne and Diana drink some "raspberry cordial." Diana gets dizzy and Anne walks her home.

10. A. Philippa Pearce: *Tom's Midnight Garden*.
    Chapter 27 — "A Talk for Tom Long."
    Tom and Hatty relive many experiences through discussion.

Discussion and Role Playing

Purpose: • To provide a context in which children may express ideas and explore possible behavior alternatives
• To foster a responsible and caring attitude

Children should be given copies of the following ideas and instructed to think about inherent value conflicts. They may wish to draw illustrations or make notes in the margin. Some of the situational conflicts may form the basis of a class discussion. Following the discussion, situations and resolutions may be dramatized by role playing. Incidents taken from daily class activities form the basis of these conflict situations. By recording incidents, you may develop your own file of situational conflicts.

1. You are having a discussion with David, John, Becky, and Diane over the interpretation of a rule in soccer. How is the problem resolved?

2. (a) A project on computers has been assigned. You discuss the topic with Leah and Allan. Sub-topics are suggested by the teacher. You attempt to convince your friends to divide the work load evenly.
   (b) The project is presented to the class. Your classmates and teacher do an evaluation. The three of you discuss results and ideas for future projects.

3. Although it is against school rules, you throw a snowball at Janey. The teacher on duty sends you to Mrs. Muir, the Vice-Principal. She is going to punish you, but tries to decide on a punishment other than suspension. You apologize and attempt to convince her that your action was harmless and unintentional.

4. Anthony's gerbil gets loose in the classroom. You and Michael help him search for it. Many students become involved and the teacher asks the students to go to their seats. You try to explain the importance of catching the gerbil immediately.

5. You've worked on a Math problem for fifteen minutes. You call Rob to get some help. The telephone conversation gets lengthy and your parents tell you it is time for bed. What do you do about the incomplete homework?

6. You work with Sheira, Jerome, and Asa to prepare a scene from *Alice in Wonderland* for dramatization. Mrs. Charney tells you there is too much noise in the project room. She states that the remainder of the class is attempting to evaluate the previous skit. Sheira pleads that noise is necessary for a successful production. How is the problem resolved?

Story Starters from Children's Literature

> **Purpose:** • **To assist children in considering personal values**
> • **To have students compare their personal writing with that of a well-known author**
> • **To encourage students to write "in the style of an author"**

The following excerpts have been taken from the indicated books. They prove successful when used as story starters.

1. Alice was beginning to get very tired of sitting outdoors with her sister, and of having nothing to do. (*Alice in Wonderland*)

2. Walking back to camp through the swamp, Sam wondered whether to tell his father what he had seen. (*The Trumpet of the Swan*)

3. When Mary Lennox was sent to Misselthwaite Manor to live with her uncle, everybody said she was the most disagreeable-looking child ever seen. (*The Secret Garden*)

4. On the second Monday of September in 1897, I was sitting on top of the world. (*Me and My Little Brain*)

5. It was warm outside and the other animals were revelling in the spring sunshine, but Meg crouched in the straw and brooded unhappily on her problems. (*Little Brother*)

6. Elizabeth is, in every way, her father's daughter. (*Elizabeth Blackwell — First Woman Doctor*)

7. There was once a velveteen rabbit, and in the beginning he was really splendid. (*The Velveteen Rabbit*)

8. There was a little boy called Eustace Clarence Scrubb, and he almost deserved it. (*The Voyage of the Dawn Treader*)

9. The island of Gont, a single mountain that lifts its peak a mile above the storm-racked Northeast Sea, is a land famous for Wizards. (*Wizard of Earthsea*)

10. This is the story of the different ways we looked for treasure, and I think when you have read it you will see that we were not lazy about the looking. (*The Story of the Treasure Seekers*)

11. Two voices, a mellow, bell-like baying and an excited yelping, came in chorus upon the air of the April dawn. (*Red Fox*)

12. The sound of the howling wind and the beating of snow on the side of the igloo told them that the weather was too hazardous to go hunting. (*Harpoon of the Hunter*)

13. If you want to find Cherry-Tree Lane, all you have to do is ask a policeman at the cross-roads. (*Mary Poppins*)

14. Young Florence Nightingale gave "Granny" Evans a gentle pat as she walked past the bed to the door of the dingy one-room cottage. (*The Lady with the Lamp*)

15. Let it be papa, Ann wished desperately as she tugged open the big front door. (*From Anna*)

16. If, standing alone on the back doorstep, Tom allowed himself to weep tears, they were tears of anger. (*Tom's Midnight Garden*)

17. The twins found the doll on a cold, wet Saturday in early spring. (*Twin Spell*)

18. My baptism is an unpleasant memory. (*Growing Pains*)

19. The tapping on the window woke him. (*A Dog So Small*)

20. Claudia knew that she could never pull off the old-fashioned kind of running away. (*From the Mixed-Up Files of Mrs. Basil E. Frankweiler*)

* * *

Sample Story I

The Lost Galleon

Starting Point: Walking back to camp through the swamp, Sam wondered whether to tell his father what he had seen. (*The Trumpet of the Swan*)

Student's Story

Walking back to camp through the swamp, Sam wondered whether to tell his father what he had seen. It seemed impossible, but Sam was sure it had happened. When he reached camp he told his father what had happened.

He said, "While I was exploring around the camp I heard some rustling in the darkest part of the swamp. I had heard tales of an old Spanish Galleon that had attacked an English town on the edge of one of the Florida Keys. The town fell to the invaders very quickly because it was unguarded. When the men had gone to England for supplies, the Spaniards stole everything of value. When their ship was loaded with supplies and treasure they tortured the townspeople and left the town in flames. The only person to survive their raid was a sorcerer who cursed them to be lost in the Florida Keys forever and become the undead.

"I decided to see if the tale was true so I climbed into my boat and rowed towards the sound and hid behind a small bush on an island. Soon I saw a large wooden ship that looked like a Spanish Galleon. I heard shouts of direction from the man in the crows-nest but I couldn't see the man or anybody else on board because of a thick fog reaching from bow to stern and from the deck to the top of the mast. When the ship passed me the fog lifted and I saw the crew for the first time. My mouth hung open because the crew was made up of pale, shrivelled-up men wearing rotted clothes and rusted armor. Suddenly the ship stopped at the island from which I was observing and four of the men came off the ship and walked towards me. Then the man in the lead spoke, 'Please tell us the way out so we can die.' I was too scared to answer so I just turned and ran, leaving the men and the boat stranded. The water wasn't over my waist so I waded back to camp and decided to tell you the story. I figure that if I'm insane you should be the first one to know.''

''Son,'' his father answered, ''if you're insane then so am I because I saw the same thing as you witnessed, fifteen years ago.''

And so the Lost Galleon still searches for the way out of the Florida Keys.

Frank Olsen,
Grade 7
Ottawa, Ontario.

Sample Story II
The Double Agent

Starting Point: It was a dark and stormy night. (*A Wrinkle in Time*)

Student's Story

It was a dark and stormy night. The shutters on the windows of the old mansion creaked and groaned. The mansion had fifty rooms and was owned by Mrs. Olga Schmidt.

Dawn was breaking. It was six o'clock and the mailman rode in his truck down the roads of highland Transylvania. He stopped in front of a large house and took several letters from his sack. He knocked on the door and a maid answered.

''I have mail for your mistress,'' he told her.

The maid ran down a long flight of stairs, down a corridor and into a large room. Her mistress sat on a large armchair, reading the morning paper.

''I have the mail for you, Madame,'' said the maid.

''Ah, thank you, Louise!'' roared Olga Schmidt.

Olga opened the first letter. Her face purpled as she read it. It read like this:

Dear Olga:

   Will you come to my house in Hamburg? I'm having trouble hiding the microfilm. Your brother, Hans.

The next morning Olga got on the train to Hamburg. When she got there, the microfilm was in a can of tuna. The cook knew which one it was, but he had quit that morning. Olga's brother had invited the mayor for dinner and he insisted on eating his favorite dish, tuna fish casserole.

The following morning Olga had a brilliant idea. She hired a doctor to operate on the mayor.

Little did she know the doctor was a double agent.

The next day the mayor was sent up and wheeled into the operating room. The doctor whispered to his nurse, "Got the microfilm case?"

The nurse nodded. She put the mayor under the anaesthetic and the operation began. After about five minutes, the doctor brought up a role of soggy microfilm. He gave it to the nurse, who put it in the microfilm case.

The doctor did not realize that his nurse was also a double agent. She switched the microfilm cases and brought one of them back to Olga and Hans. They were very pleased but they didn't know where to hid it. Finally, they decided on a bottle of ketchup. Little did they know that the Count of Transylvania, a ketchup lover, was coming for dinner tomorrow . . .

Jill Salley,
Grade 6,
Ottawa, Ontario.

Creative Writing Starters

Purpose:
- **To encourage children to think and write about topics in which personal values must be considered**
- **To promote open-mindedness**

1. I'll try again, or Starting Over.
2. Why do I have to wear glasses?
3. Sometimes I feel so awkward.
4. Why do my brothers and sisters get praise when I get punishment?
5. My teacher/parent understands the problem, but insists that I work out a solution.
6. The hockey game begins at 6:00 p.m.
7. It is Saturday, July 5, the sun is shining, and I'm feeling terrific.
8. My skiing/skating/swimming instructor is helpful in many ways.

Sample Story

Starting Over

Jimmy stared blankly at the freshly-opened report card. He was in the Sixth Grade at Carnation Park School. Minutes before, he had been running home from school and looking forward to two glorious months of summer vacation. On his report card there was but one "A"; this was for music. Two hours ago he would have given anything to have that "A"; now it didn't even bring a faint smile to his lips. His face was an expressionless mask. Suddenly he cried, "I've failed, I've failed," as he rushed up the staircase and flung himself onto his bed.

Mr. Splithers, Jimmy's father, had been working in his study and came running when he heard the noise. "What's the matter, Jim?" said Mr. Splithers as he entered the bedroom.

"Look," sobbed Jim, and he flung the report card at his father. Mr. Splithers examined the paper very carefully. Hiding his surprise, he said, "But Jim, you got an 'A' for music. You told me that was your goal for this year. You've reached your goal."

"But I failed in every other subject," Jim cried as he shook the report card which he had snatched from his father's hands.

"That makes no difference, Jim," said Mr. Splithers calmly. "Not everybody is a born genius, but I know and you know that you are a born musician. You are good at it. It's your talent!"

"You really think so?" asked Jim.

"I know so," replies Mr. Splithers. "Come, let's have a talk with your principal, right now."

Jimmy was put into an "extra help" Grade Seven classroom at his school and at the age of thirty-seven, he became the conductor of the London Symphony Orchestra and famous throughout the world. Yet, through all his glamour and fame he always remembered that day, the first time that he had really believed in himself, believed that he really was a musician.

Alex Hay,
Grade 5,
Ottawa, Ontario.

Values in Literature: Positive and Negative

Purpose:	• **To encourage critical reading**
	• **To help children appreciate books within an historical context**

The positive and negative aspects of this series of books introduce one approach teachers may take when discussing books with students. You might further discuss a moral or ethical dilemma and ask students for the values issue in the situation. This activity should help students get into the habit of thinking in terms of values and concepts as they read rather than just skimming a book for the plot or story.

Laura Ingalls Wilder Series — Positive Aspects

1. (a) power of family relationships revealed and virtues of family life presented.
   (b) individual energies are directed towards family survival and happiness (seems important at a time when many children are without this sense of family unity).

2. (a) unconditional giving (Laura becomes a teacher to get money for her sister to go to a school for the blind).

3. (a) books in series give a sense of trying to establish values on the "edge" of civilization.
   (b) certain formalities of civilization help elevate family life from mere survival (fiddle, song, dance, family discussion).
   (c) in lieu of negative "vibes" to which children resort today, songs and poetry provide resolution to daily problems.

Critical Reading — Negative Aspects

Textual examples taken from *The Long Winter*.

1. Sex-role stereotyping and racism:
   p. 4: "She did not like to see women working in the fields. Only foreigners did that. Ma and her girls were Americans, above doing men's work."

2. Racism:
   p. 64: "Ma despised Indians. She was afraid of them too."

3. Sex-role stereotyping:
   p. 78: "... girls don't play ball although some girls want to play."

p. 82: "Twice Cap Garland urged them to play ball with the boys at recess, but they stayed inside the school house and watched the game through the window."

4. Sex-role stereotyping, realism:
p. 98: "Back in York State when they were boys and later on Father's big farm in Minnesota, they had never thought of cooking; that was woman's work. But since they had come West to take up homestead claims they had to cook or starve."

Discussion Questions
Wilder's The Long Winter
(Harper Trophy, 1971 edition)

1. p. 248: "Say, that's my seed wheat and I'm not selling it!": Almanzo replied. "We're out of wheat at my house and I am buying some," Pa replied.
    Almanzo Wilder seems to display selfishness in hiding the seed wheat from the needy community. Royal Wilder encourages Almanzo to sell the wheat to make a profit.

    (a) Is Almanzo abdicating his responsibility to the community? Why?/Why not?

    (b) Is Royal a more altruistic person or is he merely considering financial gain? Support your answers with textual evidence.

2. p. 257: Almanzo risks his life to find wheat for the community. He finds and convinces Mr. Anderson to sell some wheat by arguing that it is a moral responsibility.
    p. 277: "The folks in town have got to have some of your wheat or starve." ". . . that's my seed wheat. It's my next year's crop. I could have sold it last fall if I was going to sell it."

    Discuss Almanzo's argument in light of his actions regarding his own seed wheat.

3. p. 309: "She (Laura) felt beaten by the cold and the storms. She knew she was dull and stupid but she could not wake up."
    p. 311: ". . . The blizzard was loud and furious. 'It can't beat us!' Pa said. 'Can't it, Pa?' Laura asked stupidly. 'No,' said Pa. 'It's got to quit some time and we don't. It can't lick us. We won't give up.' "
    Then Laura felt a warmth inside her. It was very small, but it was strong. It was steady, like a tiny light in the dark, and it burned very low but no winds could make it flicker because it would not give up.

    (a) What accounts for Laura's change in feeling and attitude?
    (b) Has support from family members or friends ever helped you overcome negative feelings or depression.

Wonderland Card Game

Purpose:	• **To develop decoding and interpreting skills**
	• **To promote enjoyment of reading**

Object of Game: to accumulate 50 points.
Players: 2 to 4 players, Grades 4 to 8.
Materials: a set of cards (examples given).
Skills Reinforced: — ability to synthesize information.
                    — oral literacy skills.
                    — short- and long-term memory practice.

Construction of Cards:

1. Collect 60 4" × 6" index cards. Use the cards to make two equal piles of 30.

2. Print the word "Identity" on one side of the cards in one pile. Print the word "Adventure" on one side of the cards in the second pile.

3. Collect the two stacks of 30 cards, shuffle, and distribute all the cards to the children in the class. Each student will now have 2 or 3 index cards, with the word "Identity" or "Adventure" printed on one side of the card.

4. Ask the students to refer to the "Recommended Reading List." For "Identity" each child will turn the identity card over to the blank side and print the following:
    (a)   Title of Book
    (b)   Author
    (c)   One incident from the book which affects the character's identity.

Note: (i)   Children should choose familiar books so they can merely skim the book to choose an important incident.
        (ii)   The teacher should define "incident" for students and emphasize the importance of choosing issues or incidents which are relevant to identity in a novel.
        (iii) Students may wish to supplement their chosen incident with an appropriate illustration.
        (iv)   With over two hundred books available from the "Books of the Month Reading List," and the large number of possible Incidents for each book, the probability of two students choosing the same novel and the same incident is remote.
        (v)   However, if this repetition occurs, suggest to one of the students concerned that an alternate book or incident be chosen, since only one card will be used.

5. Have students follow the same instructions in (4) above for "Adventure" card(s).

6. Collect the 60 cards. Check the cards for repetition and accuracy.

7. Examples: (Understood Betsy), (Knight's Castle), (Twin Spell), (The Painted Garden).

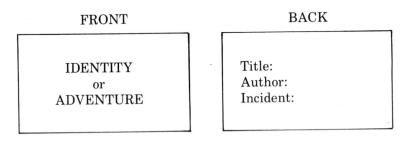

FRONT   BACK

IDENTITY   Title:
or   Author:
ADVENTURE   Incident:

4" × 6" INDEX CARD

Rules of the Game

1. Shuffle the cards and distribute three Identity and three Adventure cards to each player.

2. The person seated on the left side of the dealer begins the game by laying one of his/her cards on the table. He/she then states the title and author of the book and relates three or more events revolving around the adventure or identity crisis. Replace each card used with one from the top of the pile.

3. If the player successfully related three incidents, he or she gains 15 points. If additional, relevant points are cited, 5 extra points are given for each incident.

4. One player should have a pencil and paper to act as scorekeeper.

5. If a player is unable to relate details using the cards in his or her hand, one card may be picked up from the top of the pile and one should be discarded.

6. The first player to accumulate 50 points is the winner.

7. Another player acts as a judge to determine whether or not details given by players are relevant.

*   *   *

Card Examples: Wonderland Game

A. Understood Betsy

Adventures: Betsy and Molly find themselves deserted at the Necronsett Valley Fair.

Incidents:
1. The Wendells arrange for Betsy and Molly to get a ride home to Putney Farm with the Vaughans in their big wagon.
2. The girls check the booth for the Vaughans to find that one of their cows was sick and they had started home.
3. When Betsy and Molly realize they have been deserted, Betsy decides to act in the manner Cousin Ann would act.
4. She quiets and reassures Molly first.
5. She solves the problem by earning some money to enable them to take the train home.

B. Knight's Castle

Adventure: Children are informed they will be spending their vacation in Baltimore, Maryland, so that their father may have an operation.

Incidents:
1. Family postpones other vacation plans (Rocky Mountains, Wampler's Lake).
2. Family plans to stay with Aunt Katharine, Jack, and Eliza while in Baltimore.
3. Ann reads about Baltimore in "The American Family Encyclopedia" and Roger plays with his collection of toy soldiers.
4. Three days are spent planning and packing before the family leaves for Baltimore.
5. Vacation at Aunt Katharine's home proves interesting as the children play with model soldiers from a shop called "The Knight's Castle" in a castle which they name Torquilstone from *Ivanhoe*.

C. Twin Spell

Adventure: Elizabeth and Jane Hubbard are given an old doll at "Antiques, Dolls Mended Shop."

Incidents:
1. Girls are interested in finding out about the time or historical period from which the doll comes.

2. Father suggests they go to the library and museum. " '. . . make notes, and gather all your information before you start looking again.' 'But that's organizing,' said Elizabeth outraged."

3. The girls find out if the doll is from the 1840s; they find out about dress and homes of the time.

4. The girls use information from the following book in the research: William Sabiston, *City on the Lake, Being a Brief History of the City of Toronto, 1793–1861.*

Related Ideas:

1. Read novel. Record the steps used by the twins to find information about the doll. Use similar steps to find information about your doll, soldier, and so on.

2. Dramatize Chapter 3 — "Aunt Alice Gets a Sick-Basket," pp. 24-38.

3. Obtain models of soldiers, dolls from a museum, or have them made with costumes representing a certain time period. A drawing depicting an object from a definite time period might also be used. Give the soldier or doll to a group of students; instruct them to find out and do research on the historical period from which the doll or soldier came.

Example: — Doll in *Twin Spell.*
— Drawing from *Tom's Midnight Garden* — the Grandfather Clock.
— Models from *The Twelve and The Genii* — soldiers from the Napoleonic era.

D. The Painted Garden

Adventure: Mr. Bryan J. Brown wants to test Jane for a part in the film "The Secret Garden."

Incidents:
1. Jane runs to the beach to see the tied-up spaniel.
2. Jane sees spaniel by water eating dead fish.
3. Jane is angry, confronts dog's owner, Mr. Brown, about treatment of dog.
4. Jane learns dog is called Hyde Park as she offers to take it for a walk.
5. Mr. Brown promises to visit Jane's home and speak to her father about a business deal. Rather than the dog, he speaks to her about the possibility of her playing Mary in the film "The Secret Garden."

Related Ideas for Discussion
Discuss identity themes:
• on being important

- self-fulfillment
- self-actualization
(Rachel, Jane, John)

Plot:
- sacrifice
- move to California
- new adventures to fulfil old goals

Sub-Plot:
- filming of *The Secret Garden*
- Jane's role and identity

Discuss references in *The Painted Garden* to other children's classics:
a.   Kansas City — "Dorothy" in *The Wizard of Oz.*
b.   "Fine Reading" in *Treasure Island.*
c.   "Sub Plot" in *The Painted Garden.*

Suggested Readings

Bettelheim, Bruno. *The Uses of Enchantment.* Toronto: Random House, 1976.

Davis, Gary A. *Creativity Is Forever.* San Francisco, CA.: Badger Press, 1981.

Egoff, Sheila. *Only Connect.* New York: Oxford University Press, 1969.

Fader, Dan. *The New Hooked on Books.* New York: Berkley Publishers, 1976.

Fisher, Margery. *Who's Who in Children's Literature.* New York: Holt, Rinehart and Winston, 1975.

Graves, Donald H. *Writing: Teachers and Children at Work.* London: Heinemann Educational Books, 1983.

Grost, Audrey. *Genius in Residence.* Toronto: Prentice-Hall, 1970.

Harmir, Merrill; Kirschenbaum, Howard; and Simon, Sidney. *Clarifying Values Through Subject Matter.* Minneapolis, MN.: Winston Press, Inc., 1973.

Koch, Kenneth. *Rose, where did you get that red?* New York: Vintage Books, 1973.

Koch, Kenneth. *Wishes, Lies, and Dreams.* New York: Harper & Row, 1970.

Landau, E.; Epstein, S.; and Stone, A., eds. *The Exceptional Child Through Literature.* Englewood Cliffs, N.J.: Prentice-Hall, 1978.

Landsberg, Michele. *Michele Landsberg's Guide to Children's Books.* Markham, Ont.: Penguin Books, 1985.

L'Engle, Madeleine. *A Circle of Quiet.* New York: Seabury Press, 1979.

Lindbergh, Anne Morrow. *Gift from the Sea.* Toronto: Vintage Books, 1978.

Maid, Amy, and Wallace, Roger. *Not Just Schoolwork.* New York: Irvington Publishers Inc., 1980.

Opie, Iona and Peter. *Children's Games in Street and Playground.* Oxford: Oxford University Press, 1969.

Roeper Review 5:3 (February 1983) "Reading and the Gifted Student."

Sagoff, Maurice. *Shrink Lits.* New York: Workman Pub. Co., 1980.

Samples, Bob. *The Metaphoric Mind.* Reading, MA.: Addison-Wesley Publishing Company, 1976.

Sloan, Glenna Davis. *The Child as Critic.* Teachers College Press, Columbia University, 1975.

Vail, Priscilla L. *The World of the Gifted Child.* Pickering, Ont.: Beaverbooks, 1979.

———. *Clear and Lively Writing.* Rexdale, Ont.: John Wiley & Sons, 1981.

Veninga, James F. *The Biographer's Gift.* Texas Committee for the Humanities, 1983.

6

Perceptions

Visualizations

"Those of us who have gone down a rabbit hole, climbed the mast
of a plunging schooner with a pirate hot on our tails, . . . or have
gone far back in time on the back of a cat — those of us who
have done these things realize how narrow and bleak our lives
would have been if untouched by these mind-stretching adventures. Beyond the mere techniques and skills of learning to read
lies a land of vision and enchantment. A child who is never
pointed in that direction . . . may grow to adulthood literate in
only the 'letters' sense of the word, and with a sadly under-
nourished spirit."

Nancy Polette and Marjorie Hamlin,
Reading Guidance in a Media Age,
(Metuchen, N.J.: Scarecrow Press, 1975), p. 8.

The educative process must be both varied and innovative since no two
children learn in the same manner. The use of visualization (seeing with
the mind's eye) lies at the heart of such a philosophy for it is based upon
the principle that people do not "think" or "see" in the same fashion.

The advocacy of visualization results from the tremendous amount of
research in brain function and learning styles that has occurred in the last
decade. For example, the integrative learning approach, as outlined by Bev
Galyean in some of her writings and audiotapes, places the logical, linear,
and sequential functions of the brain within the context of its holistic, intuitive and image-based functions. By instructing teachers how to use this
integrative approach to education, we can ensure that children develop,
or at the very least maintain, the rich inner world of imagery that will
enable them to become creative producers in society, instead of passive
consumers.

Some of the basic principles which theorists apply to imagery or visualization are as follows:

1. Visualization can be taught, developed, and used in real life situations.
2. Visualization abilities vary among individuals.
3. Visualization improves with conscious use.
4. Like circle meetings and brainstorming, visualization contains no
   wrong answers.
5. Visualization is multi-sensory. The "Mind's eye" *sees* images, feels tex-
   tures, tastes foods, smells odors, and hears sounds.

As noted in the suggested readings, there are many approaches and
techniques to be used in visualization. We may look at visual thinking
exercises on the continuum suggested by Lorraine Plum, from structured
to unstructured, including receptive, suggestive, guided, and programmed. The authors' experience would suggest that the guided, suggestive, and
receptive types are the most appropriate types of visualization to be used
in the classroom setting. Visualization also can be integrated into language
arts, history, science, art, and any sort of integrated units. Samples of guid-

ed imagery occur in the following pages with exercises such as the water cycle and fantasy journeys. A creative product which incorporates imagery is explained in the write up on "Tapestry."

> "I find that words, or language, as they are written or spoken, do not seem to play any role in my mechanisms of thought. I see my thoughts in IMAGES."
>
> *Albert Einstein*

Reflections on Visualization

"The best thinking seems to integrate the two ways of knowing. By providing fantasies and our usual verbal information, we give students experience in combining these two modes of thinking and knowing."

> *G. Hendricks and T. Roberts,* The Second Centering Book *(Englewood Cliffs, N. J.: Prentice-Hall, 1977), p. 48.*

"The mind's eye, spontaneously active in dreaming, can also be consciously directed. Unlike the sensory eye, which is bound to the here-and-now, the mind's eye can travel in space and time to the here-and-then, can entertain fantasy, can form, probe, and manipulate structures and abstract ideas, can obtain insight into realities that have not been seen and can foresee future consequences of present plans."

> *Robert McKim,* Experiences in Visual Thinking *(Monterey, Ca.: Brooks/Cole Publishing Company, 1972), p. 81.*

"One of the most interesting aspects of creativity is that affective development seems to go along with cognitive development, so that positive feelings about oneself, others and the universe are felt by most creative people."

> *John Curtis Gowan,* Trance, Art and Creativity *(Buffalo, N.Y.: Creative Education Foundation, 1975), p. 306.*

"The genius of the future will be the creative mind adapting itself to the shape of things to come."

> *E. P. Torrance,* The Search for Satori and Creativity *(Buffalo, N.Y.: Creative Education Foundation, 1979), p. 9.*

Visual Imagery with Nursery Rhymes

A. Mary had a little lamb, its fleece was white as snow,
   And everywhere that Mary went the lamb was sure to go.
   It followed her to school one day, which was against the rule,
   It made the children laugh and play to see a lamb at school.
   And so the teacher turned it out, but still it lingered near,
   And waited patiently about till Mary did appear.
   What makes the lamb love Mary so? The eager children cry:
   Why Mary loves the lamb you know, the teacher did reply.

B. Twinkle, twinkle, little star,
   How I wonder what you are!
   Up above the world so high
   Like a diamond in the sky.

C. Jack and Jill when up the hill
   To fetch a pail of water;
   Jack fell down and broke his crown,
   and Jill came tumbling after.

   Then up Jack got and home did trot,
   As fast as he could caper,
   They put him to bed and plastered his head,
   With vinegar and brown paper.

          *   *   *

Visual Imagery

The title of this activity is "It followed her to school one day." Does anyone have an idea what the activity is about?

It could be about Mary and her lamb, but it doesn't have to be. When we use our imagination, we can get ideas and see anything we wish to see.

As you hear or read the poem, get ideas about details you hadn't thought about before.

From Bob Eberle, *Visual Thinking* (East Aurora, N.Y.: DOK Publishers, 1982), p. 46. Reprinted by permission of the publishers.

Probe Questions (Attending to Detail)

1. What color was Mary's dress?
2. Did Mary walk, skip, or run to school?
3. Describe Mary's schoolhouse.
4. Describe Mary's teacher.
5. Did Mary have any other animals as pets?
6. What kind of a day was it?
7. How did Mary's parents respond to the incident?
8. Would you like to be followed to school by a favorite pet? Give reasons for or against.

Thoughts and Dreams

You are in a variety of settings. What are your thoughts and dreams?

You are		
	on a tropical island.	What are you imaging?
	in a sail boat.	What are you imaging?
	at a rock concert.	What are you imaging?
	in an art class.	What are you imaging?
	in a record shop.	What are you imaging?
	in a sports shop.	What are you imaging?
	at the beach.	What are you imaging?

Imaging about Active Self

I. Formulate an image of yourself in each of the following situations. Then complete the statements with an adverb of your choice.

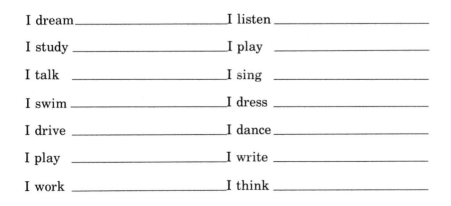

I dream_____   I listen _____

I study _____   I play _____

I talk _____   I sing _____

I swim _____   I dress _____

I drive _____   I dance _____

I play _____   I write _____

I work _____   I think _____

Dreams

Never on the surface
Bearing its soul
But in the corridors
    of your mind
It provides *Hope*.

A refuge when the rhythms of life
    tumble over you
Not unlike your mother's kiss on
    your scraped knee
Hardly a word, but the touch
    is reassuring
Inspiring you to go on.

A private room where you can be
    silly crazy,
Spontaneity flows.

A dream is a form of
    ETERNAL MUSIC
It keeps you other worldly, looking
    around the corner
You march to it, albeit silently.
But the sounds are those of a
    distant drum
You need solitude to hear them
    Utterly inspiring.
You emerge actuated by a sense of
    destiny.

A MOTIVATOR the inner life growing
    quietly
Like the unborn, yet exploding,
    vibrating
Filling you with anticipation,
Gestation must be endured.

Man, his desires, energies and
    strivings
All couple with the events of life
    and ultimately with the time of his
    maker.
Unity, man and his dream are
    harmonized, inseparable.
Thanksgiving
"My cup runneth over."

Transcending all, a dream
    gives you the indispensable COURAGE
Without which there is no growth.

Beverley Muir,
Chief Consultant for the Gifted,
North York Board of Education.

Drama, Art, and Visual Imagery

Visualize three boxes. One box should be small, one large, and one medium-sized. Put something inside of each. Draw the boxes then describe them to a friend or to the group.

Possible interpretation:
— small: inner core of self
— large: image you present to the world
— medium: creative tension

Answer each of the following sentence beginnings for each box:

1. I imagine...
2. The word that best describes me...
3. I wish...
4. I think...
5. I secretly hope...
6. I need...
7. I will...
8. I feel...
9. Assist me in...
10. Please don't describe me as...

A Guided Fantasy: Water Cycle

(From Jack Miller — *The Compassionate Teacher*, 1981)

You will be peaceful and calm throughout this fantasy. You will have a pleasant, interesting and comfortable journey. No harm will come to you at any point. You will be perfectly safe at all times. You will always be able to do whatever it is you want to do. When your experience is finished, you will feel refreshed and relaxed, peaceful and full of energy.

Allow yourself to flow with this fantasy...Let go... Give yourself permission to enter into it as completely as you can...Take your own pace...Go at your own rate.

Visualize now a large, calm lake at the base of some very high mountains... The lake is still and placid... It's dawn, and the sun is rising slowly through scattered, pink clouds... Enter into the peace and tranquility of this scene... Experience it as fully as you can... Look all around you. See everything there is to see... Listen to the early morning sounds... Smell the fresh mountain air.

Visualize the water... Now, you will BECOME the water... You will become crystal clear, pure, transparent water... You are floating . . . floating on the surface of the lake. Enjoy being there. Feel the water supporting you and buoying you up.

The rising sun's glow light penetrates the depth of your being. You are flooded with light. Let the light in... Experience the light coursing through you... Feel the sun filling your entire being with brilliant, bright light.

As the sun rises higher, you begin to feel warmer and warmer... You grow lighter and more energized... You are expanding... You begin to rise gently, invisibly floating upwards...upwards from the surface of the lake... You move higher and higher, until you are absorbed into billowy, white-gray cloud formations.

Feel yourself carried along and rolled about by friendly, pillowy clouds... Feel yourself rising with the clouds and swiftly moving upwards towards the craggy mountain peaks.

As you rise higher, a brisk, cold current of air transforms you — in an instant — into a shower of infinitely varied, brilliantly beautiful snowflakes... You move gently and ever so lightly downward towards the deep, soft snowbanks below... As you gradually descend, the bright rays of the sun pass through you, and you begin glistening and flashing with the full colour spectrum of the rainbow. Experience yourself in all your beauty and radiance.

You continue descending, lightly, airily and gracefully moving downward... Gently, gently you are cushioned by the soft snowbank and your descent is ended... Rest there in the sun and prepare for the completion of your journey... Feel the warm energy flowing through you.

Fill yourself with sunlight. Allow it to flow through your entire being... Feel the energy and power of this light... Experience its radiance... You have become a centre of light.

You are rested now and refreshed. You are ready to move on... You discover that the warm rays of the noonday sun have transformed you into crystal clear liquid... You are fluid again... You begin moving downhill... downwards towards the lake... You flow easily... now fast, now slowly... seeking your own way...feel your power as you flow.

You join other waters and move now right, now left...now over, and now under...always following the path of least resistance... Flow at your own pace and find your own way back down the lake.

You are nearing the bottom now...when you reach the lake, flow out onto the surface of the water and spread yourself out. Stretch, expand and float there. Feel the water supporting you... Enjoy the exhilaration of having completed a varied and exciting journey... Be aware of the wide range of your capabilities... Be aware of your beauty and your power.

When you are ready, come back to yourself and to this room. Keep your eyes closed... Spend some silent moments with yourself. You will feel refreshed and relaxed, energized and peaceful.

Continue to be yourself now... the person you are... and also remember that you are water. Remember your capabilities... your mobility... your power... your various modes of being... Remember that you are beautiful... Remember you are filled with energy and light... Allow yourself more often to experience yourself as fully as you have today... When you are ready, open your eyes and make some contact with this room and with the people about you.

Source: Reproduced by permission of The Confluent Education Journal, Santa Barbara, California.

Imagery Exercise I

Close your eyes and take a deep breath. You are bottled in water sensing a coolness that you've never before experienced. With you are a group of your friends. Scientists call you a school. The ocean is your playground. Merrily you follow each other through the deep, green waters — looking upward you see the sun penetrating through the surface of the water. You feel its penetrating heat warm the top of your body. The heat feels so good you slowly rise attracted to the giant yellow ball above you. Beautiful scattered light plays with your senses.

Having enough of the heat you slowly glide back towards the bottom of the lake. Feel the water tickle your nose and press against your cheeks. You rest momentarily and become lost in the swaying of some ocean plants. To and fro, to and fro, like some melodious pendulum on a clock. Confidently you wave goodbye to your friends until another day.... Slowly open your eyes and come back to us in this room.

Allan Hardy

Imagery Exercise II

Close your eyes. Breathe deeply. You have now gone back one year in time. Breathe again. We are now in the year of your birth. Breathe deeply a third time. Time is moving backwards rapidly, very rapidly.... It is the year 1725. You are in a canoe. Of what material is it made? Feel it. Describe its texture. Ahead of you sits Samuel de Champlain, the founder of New France. How is he dressed? What color is his beard, his boots?

Look around you. On your left are the banks of this mighty river. What do you see? What colors dominate this scene? Breathe in the air. How does it smell?

Splash some of the water on your face with your paddle. Taste it as it rolls off your lip. Is it salty? The river is bending to the right. Rocks pound against the side of your small canoe. Describe the sound. They are almost lost in the roar of the river. Suddenly it is quiet. There is little sound except for the noise that your paddle makes cutting through the water. Relax and enjoy the stillness of the water. When you are ready come back to us in this room...

Allan Hardy

Imagery Exercise III

You are relaxed, drifting, dreaming of slumber. Imagine your bed has become a lemon meringue pie. Sweet tangy odors nip and tease your nostrils. Small grains of sugar tickle your back, and the back of your legs. Your toes move back and forth, lost in the warm gooey meringue. Slowly you float back and forth moving with the settling of the top of the pie.

You are still asleep, breathing softly and slowly. The bed is no longer a lemon pie; instead it is a giant marshmallow. Slowly you rise and fall. Each time you roll over you are caressed by the velvety surface of the marshmallow. It's as if you were a fine jewel resting on a royal cushion.

Now imagine the bed has become a dish of soft ice cream. Slowly you roll from one side of the dish to the other until you are coated in cool, frothy ice cream. Taste the ice cream. Savor the taste as it lingers on your tongue and slowly dissolves and trickles down your throat.

Now take one last whiff of lemon, feel one more marshmallow puff, and taste the last drop of sweet ice cream. You have returned to familiar surroundings in this time and space. Slowly open your eyes.

Allan Hardy

Visual Imagery — Imagery Exercise IV

Visualize the following vignettes.

You are:
— a Chinese kite drifting through the clouds on a breezy Saturday
— cotton-candy clouds merrily dancing in the blue sky
— a spring snowman saying goodbye on a warm day
— running from school; it's three-thirty

You are:
— lapping up chocolate ice cream on a silver spoon
— a rose in the garden waking up to be kissed by the sun
— the long black shadow that's cast by the light of the moon
— closing your books; your homework's done

You are:
— the whispering rain that falls in May
— the puppy that's nuzzled; the horse that's tamed
— an ocean blue swimming pool on the hottest of days
— feeling good; there's time for one more game

You are: YOU

Allan Hardy

Fantasy Voyage

This "movie-in-the-mind" was used as an introduction to a short story for a grade 7 English class. The story was called "The Birth of an Island" and was a documentary done in diary form describing the eruption of a volcano and the scientific work done on a newly formed island off the coast of Iceland. I found that by taking the students on a voyage and letting them imagine the volcanic eruption themselves, they responded extremely well to the rather dry narrative and consequently learned more from the story.

I used the James Galway version of a *Pachelbel Canon* as music for the voyage.

*   *   *

Imagine yourself floating...floating in the middle of the warm blue, blue sky. You're all alone...drifting on a soft, puffy, billowing white cloud — floating aimlessly and lazily along. As you continue to move slowly through the sky, you glance down far below and realize that you are above the ocean. The vast blue-green water stretches on and on as far as you can see in any direction. There is nothing else but the magnificent still expanse of water — no land, no ships, just silence...you, the cloud, the blue sky and the ocean.

As you look down you suddenly notice in the distance that the water is beginning to swirl around and bubble and boil up. Small waves are beginning to form all around this one area of the ocean. As you watch the blue-green water turns a strange brown color as it continues to bubble and boil more furiously than before, and the waves grow higher and higher.

All at once — in the middle of the bubbling waves, you see a fire burning and suddenly a huge, thick column of black smoke gushes forth and rises swiftly up into the blue sky... high, high up — boiling and twisting and billowing on up — even about your cloud. Flashes of light flare through the black column as sparks of fire climb the spiral of smoke. The heat is very intense from where you are and you look down at the ocean and realize that the surging water is boiling hot. Gradually the restless brown water is pushed aside by a thick red substance that spreads out, splitting the ocean apart. Suddenly, a mound of earth pushes above the water and you realize it is the mouth of a volcano. What you have been seeing is its eruption! In the middle of the ocean...an under-water volcano.

Soon it stops spewing out smoke and fire and as you watch the red lava cools and stops flowing. The molten rock begins to harden and cool forming solid land. The ashes from the smoke settle around the volcano, building up the land around it. There is no more smoke, no more fire — the volcano has cooled, but what was once a part of the ocean is now an island. You have watched the birth of an island! Your cloud has begun slowly to descend and you hover close to the newly formed piece of land. Slowly, slowly — breathe deeply — and come back to us in this room. When you are ready, open your eyes.

Laurie Graham,
Student, York University.

Fantasy Journey

It is a warm autumn day. You decide to go for a walk in the forest. On the way you notice how all the leaves have already changed their colors and have begun to fall.

When you arrive at the forest you see red ones, yellow ones, orange and gold; they form a multi-colored carpet on the ground where you walk. This leafy carpet is soft and you playfully kick the leaves into the air as you go. Around you, you see all kinds of forest animals — rabbits, squirrels, chipmunks, and mice darting in and out between the trees. You see a racoon and follow it for awhile. It leads you through the bush, around the tree trunks and over the river until it finally disappears behind some rocks. You search and search but you cannot find it so you decide to have a rest.

You are tired.

Slowly you lower yourself onto the ground and curl up at the foot of a tree. You fall into a deep sleep.

You dream that you are a small seed floating along with the wind. It picks you up and carries you through the air. Higher and higher up in the air you go, and then slowly, slowly you begin to descend to the earth.

Gently you fall on a soft bed of autumn leaves. As you lie there you feel other leaves begin to fall upon you. Layers and layers build up forming a colorful blanket for you to snuggle under. It is so warm under your cozy blanket of leaves.

You hardly even notice that as time goes by, the days grow colder and a touch of frost nips the air. By the time the snowflakes begin to fall from the sky you are fast asleep.

The snow only adds to your covering, forming a thick white quilt on top of your blanket of leaves.

You sleep for a long, long time. Quietly undisturbed. It is so peaceful where you lie, so quiet.

One day you slowly wake up. Music is playing all around you. It is the sounds of song birds happily chirping to their young. Also the forest animals are chattering and welcoming spring.

A trickle of water makes its way slowly across your forehead. You wonder what it is and then you realize that it is the melting snow. The winter has passed and the spring sun is melting all the frozen earth. As more and more water seeps down into the soil, you decide it is time to move out.

But you cannot. You are prevented from seeing the warm spring sun by the layer of leaves which covers you.

You are too weak to move yet. Your muscles are tight and your body is cramped from lying curled up all winter.

So slowly you unwind. You stretch out your long white roots and extend them into the soil. Deeper and deeper they go searching for food and nourishment. When they discover some they suck it and pass it to your stomach.

It feels good. It has been such a long time since you have eaten. Now at last you begin to feel strong and energetic.

You feel strong enough to risk sticking your neck out to reach the sun. Higher and higher you stretch, up, up, pushing your head through the soil and leaves which try to bar your way.

You are determined to feel the warmth and light of the sun on your face. Even now you can feel its rays piercing through the leaves.
It is a long hard journey but you are determined to make it. Even though your neck gets tired, you know you will not give up. Push, push, just a little bit harder, push.

Finally you make it.

As you glide slowly through the last bit of soil, you experience a sense of triumph and you are amazed at the beauty all around you. The tiny flowers are swaying in the wind and the singing birds are building their nests in the trees. The scampering chipmunks are playing in the moss and the nearby brook is sparkling in the sunshine. Everything is alive. Yes, everything including you! You take a deep breath and let the air out slowly just feeling very thankful for the gift of life and growth.

You begin to grow more. Each day your neck grows longer forming a delicate stem for your beautiful head.

Each day you push your head higher, higher up, into the sky.

At the same time your body growns wider and your roots grow longer pushing to draw up the nourishment from the soil.

Eventually arm-like branches sprout out of your sides and these too grow thicker and stronger as the days go by.

In time, little buds form on your branches and these open up into leaves. Soon there are hundreds of beautiful deep-green leaves covering you.

Birds come and now build nests in your arms. Squirrels play in the hollows of your branches. Chipmunks chase each other around your trunk, and many other woodland animals huddle underneath you when it rains.

You provide both shade and shelter.

You are the most important part of the forest. You are a tree.   You will live on and on withstanding all kinds of storms and enduring every season. Only you will keep on growing more beautiful every day.

Your majestic arms will reach out higher and higher to the sun.

Always be glad of who you are. Always remember that you are strong; you are beautiful and you are useful. Remember that people and animals need you and love you and depend on you for many things.

Never give up. No matter how windy it gets, how wet or cold outside, always remember that you are strong and you can do anything you want to do. You pushed your way up through the soil, didn't you? You are very brave.

Always remember that.

Always remember your power and influence. And always be willing to share and to help others.

Always

    Always

      Always

Even after this journey ends — not yet, but very soon- remember all that you are: YOU ARE STRONG, YOU ARE BEAUTIFUL, YOU ARE NEEDED, AND YOU ARE BRAVE.

Then when you are ready, let yourself return. First come back to lying in the forest. Stay there for awhile. Relax. Let the cool firm soil beneath you cushion your body.

Breathe deeply. Let the peace of the forest relax you. Then slowly, very slowly, open your eyes and join our class once again.

Yvonne Sybring,
Student, York University.

A Tapestry of Love

By definition the word "tapestry" implies a form of weaving in which contrasting colors and fibres are used to produce an aesthetically pleasing sign. In essence then, unity is created through diversity.

The educational "tapestry," specifically the idea of integrated unit study, is quite similar. Students are presented with a variety of theme-related materials: audio-tapes, poems, songs, stories, movies, and so forth. From these items a common element is extracted and it becomes the central focus of the "tapestry." Such a focus may be expressed by employing an open-ended question, a question which is answered in the final stages of the study. Brainstorming techniques are conducted and from this exercise students choose a limited range of activities which will be explored. It is this latter procedure which uncovers the diverse strands which are eventually woven together to create the "tapestry."

The process of weaving can be varied, yet direction in this area is vitally important. Charts which enable appropriate data collection are generally quite useful. Another method of maintaining topic focus is the employment of "connectors" — specific criteria into which all the diverse strands must be woven.

As with any unit study, evaluation is an important aspect of the "tapestry" concept. Once again a wide range of opportunities exist. The simplest form of evaluation would be the student determining the level of quality and enjoyment provided by the "tapestry" itself. Other more tangible evaluation techniques could include the design of a media product.

The integrated "tapestry" unit offers many potential benefits. Specifically, it allows users a structural methodology and yet simultaneously allows for flexibility in both interests and styles.

Sample "Tapestry" Unit

The prototype Tapestry unit on "Love" was developed by consultant and teacher working with an Intermediate class for a period of six weeks. Approximately twenty-five hours of classroom time were devoted to this project.

One of the natural concerns of students in this age group is the idea of relationships. Thus it was mutually agreed upon that the Tapestry theme for this unit would be "Love." Subsequent to this decision students were exposed to the film, "Love Story," the CHFI (Toronto) radio program "Tapestry," the poem "I Love You," the song "The Universal Soldier," and a scholastic unit on "The Family."

After discussion and selection, students posed the question, "In what ways can love affect you as a person?" A group brainstorming session provided many responses to the question, including romantic, familial, materialistic, spiritual, universal, platonic, affection, mature love, pantheism, narcissism, and puppy love. Through activities the students explored ideas dealing with these types of love and finally chose romantic, platonic, familial, and universal — as the specific types of love to be presented in an audio-tape.

Students in the class were divided into four groups and rotated each week so that they not only gained overall thematic exposure, but were allowed the opportunity to deal with prose, poetry, music, and art. The "art" component dealt with art history, and the designing of a graphic sleeve for the final product, an audio-tape.

Facilitators provided numerous books of poetry, prose, and art history deemed necessary for further exploration and research. Record albums and audio-tapes, as well as books, were contributed by students.

Participants in the study were given classification charts and notebooks to record names and sources of materials that they felt might be used in the final product.

Near the end of the unit, each of the four groups presented its collection of materials. Decisions were made on what selections best illustrated the definitions of the four types of love. Some of the criteria used for choosing the final audio selections included: (1) appropriateness to defined types of love, (2) variety, (3) lyrical content, (4) rhythm and flow.

A radio script was prepared, melding the music, prose, and poetry selections together and with the assistance of a radio producer, the final tape was recorded. The intended audience included classes in other schools and selected radion stations.

Extended Activities

Work through a unit (approximately six weeks duration) on any theme concerned with affective development. Sample unit on love is included.

Students could engage in imagery exercises as introductory activities or as activities used to further theme development.

Story "The Day I Gave Jane the Diary" — David Lewis

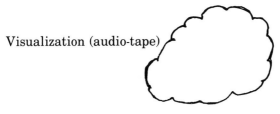

Visualization (audio-tape)

Poem: "I Like You"

Unit on "The Family"
(Scholastic)

Film: "Love Story"

CHFI Tapes — "Tapestry"

Song: "Universal Soldier"

1. New York
2. Emotion
3. California
4. Crime

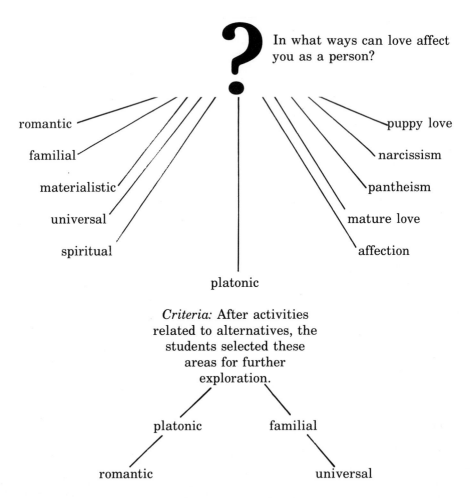

? In what ways can love affect you as a person?

romantic

familial

materialistic

universal

spiritual

platonic

puppy love

narcissism

pantheism

mature love

affection

Criteria: After activities related to alternatives, the students selected these areas for further exploration.

platonic

familial

romantic

universal

137

Resource Sheets

GROUP: _____   DATE: _____

Literary Work	Resource	Author	Page/Cut	Availability

Source: Brandy Horler, Resource Teacher, Dufferin County Board of Education.

138

Data Collection

ROMANTIC	PLATONIC	FAMILIAL	UNIVERSAL

— cross classification chart — using types of love and
(a) definition
(b) poems
(c) prose selections
(d) songs
(e) art

Data Collection

	ROMANTIC	PLATONIC	FAMILIAL	UNIVERSAL
Definition	• a strong passionate affection for a person of the opposite sex	• a warm liking • a tender feeling	• hold dear • devotion	• brotherhood and sisterhood
Poems	2• "How Do I Love Thee" — E. B. Browning • "Her Answer" — J. Bennett • "Le Demi Jour"	• "I Like You" — Unknown	• The Nortons	
Prose Selections	• "The Rosy World of Romance" — History — 1900-1910	• "What Are Friends?" — (Starting Point in Reading — AI)	• "Family" H. Christensen (Scholastic Unit)	• The Rubaiyat of Omar Khayyam (translated by E. Fitzgerald)
Songs	• "Perhaps Love" — J. Denver • "The Rose" — B. Midler • "Une Rose Pour Isabelle" — R. Whittaker	• "You've Got A Friend" — C. King • "I Love Little Baby Ducks" — T. T. Hall	• "Living Together" • "When I Am 64" —Beatles • "Daniel — My Brother" — Elton John • "Father & Son" — Cat Stevens	• "Butterscotch Castle" — Captain & Tennille • "All You Need Is Love" — Beatles

Data Collection
Choice of Songs for Program

We will make an audio-tape for airing on radio stations and write "connectors" using the following criteria:

(a)   fit into types
(b)   variety of genre of music, poetry
(c)   hear lyrics
(d)   rhythm — variety
(e)   order — two works which flow or fit together.

Assessing the Conclusion

It is possible to use the above criteria to select songs, prose, and poetry for integration into the audio-tape. Art products could be used for tape cover.

Product

(audio-tape for local radio stations)

Evaluation

1. Activity was enjoyed by all students in Grade 8 class.
2. Final broadcast group was selected on talent basis. This was productive but difficult in that all the students contributed to the product and were anxious to be a part of the final group.
3. Tape is being requested and used by many classes and resource personnel throughout Ontario.
4. There were many exciting integrated activities being done in conjunction with this effort.
    (a)   A communications and guidance unit on "Family" was completed.
    (b)   The Love-ly Musical Revue was performed at a spring concert at school. Students presented the most popular love songs from the decades of the twentieth century. Choreography and dramatic techniques were used to enhance the production.
5. The final audio-tape was rather mellow in mood. We questioned this result and concluded that this largely resulted from the fact that throughout the unit we played selections from CHFI's "Tapestry" which are purposefully mellow in mood.
6. The CHFI tape on "Love" may be compared to the audio-tape prepared by students.

Any theme may be chosen by students and teacher. If resources are available, it may be meaningful to divide students into groups and let them pursue a topic of interest.

Please note that many alternatives are available to teachers and students. Resources may be chosen according to particular interests.

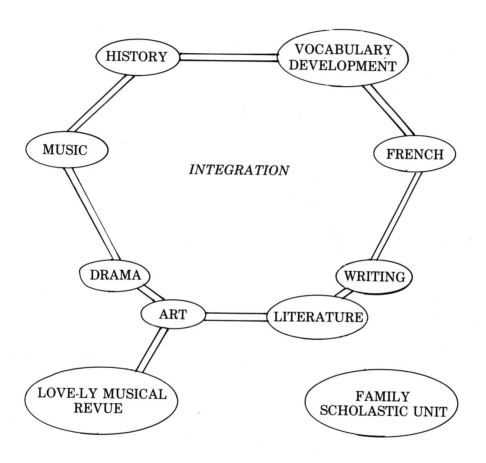

LOVE-LY MUSICAL REVUE

		INTRODUCTION	SELECTIONS	ACT
1900-1920	1.	Being in love and the joys and sorrows of this condition has been the theme of many songs over the ages	In A Canoe	— 3 boys — 1, 2, 3, vaudeville routine
			You Are My Sunshine	— harmony
	2.	The Intermediate Choir and Grade 8s would like to present to you a selection of love songs of the 1900s.	Let Me Call You Sweetheart Down By the Old Mill Stream	— 3 couples act out story line
	3.	We will begin with some golden-oldies of the first two decades of this century.	Five Foot Two	— 3 boys dance
1930-1940	4.	The '30s and '40s were the years of the Depression and World War II. Love, both for that special person and for one's country, was tested, but managed to survive.	Side By Side K-K-K-Katy Don't Sit Under the Apple Tree Edelweiss Que Sera Sera	— 6 girls tramp chorus line — 3 soldiers around campfire — 1 girl, 1 boy act out as dream — harmony — whole choir introduction
1950s	5.	You probably need no further introduction to the 1950s when the love affairs were with rock 'n roll and the jive.	Hound Dog Bye Bye Love	— Elvis dance — played by Rock 'n Roll Band 3 guitars and 1 drum — 2 couples jiving routine

1960s	6.	The 1960s brought a new generation of love songs. They expanded the meaning of life beyond the personal and romantic to feelings about all people, humankind, the problems of life, and the need for tenderness.	Get Together Terre D'Amour Can't Buy Me Love	— sung by 8 hippies in front of choir — peace signs — whole choir (French) — Beatles imitation and screamers
1970s	7.	Neither the adoration of the Fabulous Four from Liverpool nor the back-to-nature theme of the hippies proved to solve all the problems caused by our rapidly developing technology. The love songs of the 1970s began to reflect the increasing cynicism and disillusionment.	Time in a Bottle What Do You Get When You Fall in Love? Love is Blue	— choir — Instrumental band played — 1st verse — boys — 2nd verse — girls — 3rd verse — all & choir — in French & English
1980s	8.	The 1980s have "only just begun", so it is difficult to identify a trend in love songs. It is our hope that from the roots, seeds, and thorns of the past, a healthy attitude towards love will grow.	The Rose	— whole choir sings — 4 girls in black — mime routine down stage

Prepared by: Brandy Horler, Resource Teacher, Dufferin County Board of Education.

Futures and Imagery

> **Purpose:** • **To encourage critical and creative thinking about personal and global futures**

It is important for gifted children to visualize the future and their role in it. Leadership for global futures can be an exciting area of study for the gifted.

A multi-phased futures project, organized for Dufferin County students, explores values and visionary ideals. It entails a ''Futures Symposium'' in a central Board location, a one-week ''Futures Conference'' exploring personal futures and creative problem-solving and a conference examining ''Leadership for Global Futures'' at EPCOT Centre in Florida.

While participating in these ventures, gifted children further their abilities in imagineering, decision-making, and creative problem-solving.

The following imagery exercise can be used as a starting point. Journal writing, future circles, scenario writing can increase the creative output of the students.

Sample student writings from these projects and experiences have been included for teacher use and student inspiration.

*   *   *

Visual Imagery
Future Vision

Close your eyes, take a deep breath, and relax, I want you to think about the year 2020. How old are you? I want you to pretend that this is morning, and in your imagination you will be waking up to the year 2020. Focus on how you are waking up. Is there an alarm? Flash or light? Are you living alone? In your imagination, you are opening your eyes in your room. What does it look like? Is there a family? You stretch and get out of bed, look around your room, what does it look like? You go to the closet to get something to wear. We no longer have cottons and wools, but synthetics. What do your clothes look like? What colors are popular? You go to the bathroom. You look in the mirror. Carefully, what do you look like? Your hair, your face. Do you wear glasses? You brush your teeth from a faucet that comes out of the wall. You brush your hair. You go down the stairs towards the kitchen, and you can already smell the aroma of freshly brewed coffee — that has been programmed into your kitchen home computer, and timed to be ready at this time. In the kitchen, as you sip your coffee and take a breakfast pill, you focus in on the huge video screen that has the news on. What are the topics that are being shown? What is happening in the world news? Is there still a fear of nuclear war? What does the broadcaster look like? You prepare to leave for work, by collecting your briefcase, filled with video discs. You leave your house, step out into the street. What does it look like. You step onto the moving sidewalk, and soon onto your mass transit hovercraft. It is extremely crowded, and people are watching their wrist televisions. You arrive at work and insert your special I.D. card into a box-like contraption beside the door. It gives you permission to enter the building, and any messages that may have been collected are relayed to you. A friend has called. You enter your office. You do not have a secretary. Your office has four computers. You now work only four days per week. How do you get paid? The day continues. Focus on what you do, who you relate with.

Now, it is time to go home. You enter your doorway and smell dinner. You have previously programmed this delicacy to your kitchen computer from your office. You sit down to relax and focus in on the video screen in your living room. Sports is the feature. What are you watching? What type of sports do they have? Do we still have hockey, and football? What type of sports do you prefer now. Your pet is around you. What types of pets do we have in the year 2020? Do we still have cats and dogs? Do we still have to train them? Relax. Get the feeling of what your life is like? Are you happy? Take a deep breath. When you are ready, open your eyes and come back to us in this room.

Lil Lahe,
Teacher of the Gifted,
York Region Board of Education.

*　　　　　*　　　　　*

Sample Student Writings from Futures Projects

The Journey

Journey fast
through space
time
and life.

146

Journey through
what
has been
and
what
will be.
Let
your imagination
take you
through the future
to
places
where the limits
of linear
measurement
are not
known
and
thought
has no
bounds.

Kate Baillie,
Grade 9,
Orangeville, Ontario.

Future Train

We're all on a
non-stop train,
going nowhere,
going everywhere.

The speed varies,
Yet is the same.

It runs forever,
and a day.

For the destination
is tomorrow,
and the driver
is Fate.

Margaret Thompson,
Grade 11,
Orangeville, Ontario.

Values

We used to value horses
Now we value cars
Later we might value interplanetary trails
We used to value guns
Now we value bombs
Later we might value survival.

Kirby Pilch,
Grade 7,
Orangeville, Ontario.

The Future

A great unknown, filled with hopes and dreams
It seems so far away, yet tomorrow is a part of it,
We imagine ourselves in the future,
Older, wiser, and happier.
Excitingly we make plans
Deciding on future careers and lifestyles
We list our goals and dreams,
Our hopes and aspirations
In order to make the most of our future

Excitement fills me as I think of the future and achieving my goals

Everyday brings me a step closer.

Pam Beardsell,
Grade 11,
Mississauga, Ontario.

Futures

Science is lasers
Unknown is aliens
Money is communications
Future is power
Space is investigation
Life is death
Death is life!

Melanie Bevan,
Grade 6,
Orangeville, Ontario.

Mind Trek

The Mind, The final frontier. These are the voyages of U.S.S. Figment. His five day mission is to seek out new ideas and unchartered areas of thought. He is to boldly think what no person has thought before. A difficult and challenging mission!

Scott Vance
Grade 11,
Mississauga, Ontario.

The Prize

Trickle, Trickle
Says the gentle rainfall,
As it mixes with my tears.
Dripple, Dripple
Say my tears as they fall
And recall all the passed years.

The rain has stopped
And a fight, I have fought
Over my life with the waves
But I have lost.
And must pay the cost
And give to the sea its prize.

Patty Glassford,
Grade 10,
Orangeville, Ontario.

Potential

Most people do not know the great potential of their minds. Your mind can do almost anything you want it to do ... if you know how to make it. It is your slave, and no one can deprive you of your imagination.

Mike Brenneman,
Grade 9,
Orangeville, Ontario.

Dreams

The long nights I've spent awake in bed;
Thinking of things I'd like to do,
Thinking of things I really dread.
These dreams, they've made me realize
My life will soon be changed,
That there will come a day
When I must leave my home,
And venture far away.

I think I'd like to see some places
Where different faces I would see.
I'd travel to the Orient
And Africa, and the Mediterranean Sea.
I'd like to go to Australia,
To see the Koala Bears.
But I'd have to find a special place
And build my homestead there.

I'd build a home so fancy
It would be just right for me.
I'd plan every corner by myself,
I'd plant every flower and every single tree.
Nature would play a major part in my plans.
You cannot change what God has given this land.
Man-made things are nice,
But nature's even better.

I'd have to get a job,
To keep my candle of life burning long.
If I were ever idle,
I'd be like a boring, unfinished song.
But, first comes my education,
It seems like millions of years
Until I get out of school to see
The big world of happiness and tears.

My dreams, right now, are many.
And only dreams they are.
To reach my goals, I must work hard,
Try my best, and reach out far.
I have to make the future near
And help the time go fast.
I must reach my goals for me.
Not others, present or past.

Marnie McIntosh,
Grade 10,
Orangeville, Ontario.

Realization

Sometimes
life gets so
out of focus.
Things seem to be going
so well,
perfect,
couldn't be better.
And then,
suddenly,
without warning,
without really even changing,
a sudden realization hits,
and things become,
so awful,
terrible.
It also works the other way.
While things can seem
so messed up,
out of place,
troubles.
Suddenly,
a lot of good,
comes out of
a seemingly disastrous
situation.
The two can be combined,
and continuously alternated.
Where would it all end?

This is my realization following the Epcot Experience CPSI '86.

Greg Coles,
Grade 11,
Orangeville, Ontario.

Journal Entry

(Following the explosion of the Challenger Space shuttle)

This morning I slept in until 8:00 a.m. Marni and Patty couldn't get me out of bed.

We ate an enormous breakfast and then went into the Lampliter room for class with Sid Parnes. We left at 10:35 to see if we could catch the space shuttle go up. We waited for about 10 minutes, took some pictures and went back inside.

It was *very* cold last night — the coldest day this year — below zero.

The shuttle was delayed until 11:00 a.m. so we went outside again and I saw it just taking off and started to yell and tell everyone the direction.

We all stood around taking photographs and then the shuttle seemed to disappear. The clouds billowed up and the tow jets used during the launch sort of zoomed around crazily in the sky. I didn't realize what had actually happened. There were clouds billowing from where the shuttle had gone up. It had disappeared but I thought that was because it had gone up too fast and I had just missed it. Then I realized that the jet stream hadn't continued up where the shuttle should have gone.

We turned around and started walking back across the parking lot. Judy came up to us and asked if we knew what had happened and we said no. She then told us that the shuttle had exploded. We couldn't believe it. We had watched 7 people die and taken pictures. A man turned up the radio in his car and we heard the NASA broadcast of what had happened.

Then I clued in to all the little things I had not understood while watching the launch go up.

It was the most terrible thing that had ever happened to me. After listening to the broadcast, I turned around and Mrs. Dixon told me that it was okay and I started to cry, hard. It was terrible. Then everyone was crying.

I don't really feel like writing anymore.

I want to forget it for a while.

Lara Swift,
Grade 11,
Orangeville, Ontario.

'Twas the Night before Epcot

'Twas a hot summer night when we flew in,
Only two hours late and full of vim
To our rooms we did go,
In the morning we would flow.

We learned to use our imagination,
From Dr. Parnes of the Creative Foundation.
On the day of the shuttle's flight we saw,
Its terrible malfunction from afar.

Our future careers we did explore,
With our imagination we did much more.
The week has been a great success,
Too bad this room is such a mess!!!

Rob Lyttle,
Grade 11,
Mississauga, Ontario.

152

A Quest

Something that I would find useful would be the ability to retain more of the subconscious thought processes because my imagination is frustratingly complex, vivid, and colourful. The transfer from abstract to concrete form tends to eliminate many of the best points. When new ideas are needed, the dream can be recreated, but the beautiful substance of which the dream is made becomes more and more like the rough, concrete form that first went on paper.

Blair Smith,
Grade 11,
Mississauga, Ontario.

Imagination

When imagination lends itself to reality, the result is an image — a picture of a possibility. When imagery lends itself to life, the result is a better self — a more insightful you and the future.

Kate Baillie,
Grade 9,
Orangeville, Ontario.

C.P.S. Ho!

We came to Florida to grow
Our famous chant was "C.P.S. Ho!"
We opened our minds which began to flow
And learned things Sid wanted us to know.

It was fun and sessions were great
Barb urged us to participate
Our ideas we did facilitate
Even though we had stayed up late.

We learned to create dreams in our minds
And out future plans did we find
From our heads ideas were mined
And as a group our thoughts did bind.

C.P.S. is a wonderful thing
To our lives future plans it does bring
And if we keep it under our wing
Life will never lose its zing.

THE BEGINNING

J. Douglas Johnstone,
Grade 11,
Mississauga, Ontario.

Annotated Bibliography on "Visualization" and "Imagery"

"The Power of Images"
Sherman, Vivian
Viewpoints, 53, 3 (May 1977), pp. 1-4

The Compassionate Teacher
Miller, John
1981 — Prentice-Hall, Englewood Cliffs, N.J.

This book focuses on how certain perspectives and methods can be used so that teachers feel more at ease with themselves and with their students. The author calls this state of inner and outer harmony, "the compassionate service level of consciousness." One chapter is devoted to the theoretical discussion and inclusion of practical examples of imagery exercises. These may be used as a means of transpersonal development and as a means of reaching our "Centre."

Integrative Learning
Galyean, Beverly
1980 — Ken Zel Consultant Services, 767 Gladys Ave., Long Beach, Ca. 90804.

This audio-tape presents a case for incorporating the affective component into education since all learning has an emotional component. The lecturer gives an overview of approaches in psychological and interesting aspects of psychophysics. Parts of research studies are cited in an attempt to show the positive correlation between the effects of exercises, such as guided imagery, and the motivation to learn the basics in a variety of subject areas.

"Imagery: An Over-Looked Ability among the Gifted"
Roodin, Paul
Roeper Review, Vol. 5, No. 4 (April — May 1983) pp. 5-6

This article describes how imagery can be useful in the development of memory, thinking skills, and career decisions. Specific reference is made to the adolescent.

Educational Imagery, Strategies to Personalize Classroom Instruction
Richardson, Glenn E.
1982 — Charles C. Thomas, Publisher

This book outlines how educational imagery can be employed to help both secondary school and college students apply their imaginations in a constructive manner. Teacher–student scenarios are used to illustrate the author's claims that there are four types of imagery, including consequence imagery and simulation imagery. Some methods of educational imagery, applicable to elementary school children, are outlined in a final chapter as are methods of evaluating student reactions to these strategies.

"Developing Creativity in Gifted Children"
Lowery, Joyce
Gifted Child Quarterly, Vol. 26, No. 3 (Summer 1982), pp. 133-39

A comparative study between gifted students in a music and imagery training program and gifted students in two packaged programs: New Directions in Creativity Basic and New Directions in Creativity Enhanced. Results show the former group as scoring higher on indices of figural originality, figural fluency, figural flexibility and figural elaboration.

The Creatively Gifted Child
Khatena, Joe
1978 — Vantage Press

This author cites a number of "familiar tales" about children who are creatively gifted. After this sort of informal identification, Khatena presents an overview of tests and models used when dealing with intelligence and creativity. Numerous activities to stimulate creative thinking are noted. Many of the activities make use of analogies and the imagery process.

"An Imagery Exercise in Self-Awareness and Literary Sensitivity
Roncelli, Janet M.
April, 1980

This paper implies that for students to interpret the imagery of literature they must first have an awareness of the self. Students begin by describing themselves in both words and actions and then proceed with a greater awareness of how imagery may be communicated.

"Identification and Stimulation of Creative Imagination Imagery"
Khatena, Joe
Journal of Creative Behaviour, Vol. 12, No. 1 (1st Quarter 1978), pp. 30-38

The identification and stimulation of creative imagery is discussed.

"Genesa as an Aid to Incubation/Imagery"
Bruch, Catherine
Gifted Child Quarterly, Vol. 23, No. 4
(Winter 1979), pp. 778-91

This article applies the Genesa model (a life-sized model of the geometry of a biological cell) to the creative process. The incubation phase is especially emphasized.

"The Nature of Imagery in the Visual and Performing Arts"
Khatena, Joe
Gifted Child Quarterly, Vol. 23, No. 4 (Winter 1979), p. 735-47

The author outlines the ways in which visual imagery is necessary in the visual and performing arts and how both areas may be further developed.

He Hit Me Back First
Fugitt, Eva D.
1983 — Jalmar Press, California

This book brings together imagery and psychosynthesis techniques. It presents exercises for classroom use which attempt to promote integration of the physical, emotional, spiritual, and mental aspects of the self. Chapter 3, which is titled "Creative Imagination", incorporates imagery exercises into creative writing, personal journals, goal setting, drama, and discussion activities.

Scamper (Games for Imagination Development)
Eberle, Robert E.
1977 — D.O.K. Publishers, East Aurora, N.Y.

In this book, Osborn's ideation technique expressed by the acronym "scamper" is combined with the imagery process to enhance creative use of imaginative talent. A variety of exercises are given for children to explore.

"Maps as Schema for Gifted Learners"
Mastropieic, Marso A.: Scrvess, Thomas E.
Paper presented at the Annual Convention of the American Psychological Association, August 1982
Journal: RIE October 1983

A series of experiments was conducted with academically precocious children, all in junior high school. Results of the experiments indicated that spatially organized maps facilitated the recall of related prose material significantly more than list maps and prior presentation as well as posterior presentation.
   A secondary result showed that students in spatially organized conditions were able to most accurately reconstruct map features.

"Answers from the Unconscious"
Crampton, Martha
Synthesis 2, 1 (1978), pp. 140-151

This article outlines a mental imagery technique in which you formulate a question, address it to one's unconscious and allow the answer to erupt in the form of a mental image. It can be used to enhance one's self-understanding and to become a better problem-solver.

Project ALPHA (Advanced Learning Program in the Humanities and Arts): Creativity in Filmmaking — A Unit
Le Stontic, Anthony J.
Montgomery County Intermediate Unit 23, Blue Bell, PA., 1980.

Five lessons designed for senior high gifted and creative students. The unit focuses upon the uses of creativity in film production and covers the following topics: color, dialogue, score, angles and shots, critique, creative imagery, and creative assignment.

"Art and the Image of the Self"
Feldman, Edmund B.
Art Education, 29, 5 (September 1976).

This article examines how self-imagery is influenced by cultural factors and norms and the impact upon art education.

Poetry Therapy: A Bibliography
California State University, 1979

A diverse collection of words which outline the uses of poetry as a therapeutic tool.

Imagery: A Different Way of Thinking
Seyba, Mary E.
1984 — Educational Impressions

This book of practical exercises on developing creativity through imagery uses the notion of "the photographer inside your head" to help students visualize and complete tasks. Torrance's creative processes (fluency, flexibility, originality, elaboration) are outlined at the beginning to suggest appropriate goals for student attention and achievement.

"Imagery and Intuition: Keys to Counselling the Gifted, Talented, and Creative."
Ostrom, Gladys
Creative Child and Adult Quarterly, Vol. 6, No. 4 (Winter 1981), pp. 227-33

An outline of how to conduct an imagery workshop.

Stress Management in Gifted Education
Smith, Kim Stevens
April 1984

This annotated bibliography examines the nature and effects of stress, with emphasis upon gifted students. A glossary containing its effect upon gifted children, and stress management techniques (relaxation, imagery, and time management are presented). Annotations are arranged alphabetically and one separate chapter examines the six recommendations made for incorporating stress management and gifted education.

Guided Imageries Kids Love
(Age 10 — Adult) Parts 1 and 2
(Age 5 — 10)
—Galyean, Beverly
1980 — Ken Zel Consultant Services

These audio-tapes provide relaxation and imagery exercises to be completed by the listener, sample exercises include "colors", "problem-solving," and "emotional imagery."

Visual Imagery: A Means for Improving Self-Concept Evaluation. Major
T.; Cooper, Muriel F., 1973

A study which analyses the effect of visual imagery as a learning tool for
culturally disadvantaged children between the ages of 9 and 11. Using the
Piers-Harris Children's Self-Concept Scale and both experiment and control groups. The following findings were noted:
(1) improved self-concept in the experimental group;
(2) improved personal and group relationships;
(3) improved self-expression;
(4) increased class attendance;
(5) more established behavior patterns.
As a result of the test the authors conclude that the usage of visual imagery
be expanded.

"Vividness of Imagery and Creative Self-Perceptions"
Khatena, Joe
Gifted Child Quarterly, Vol. 19, 1 (Spring 1975), pp. 33-37

"Cosmetic Behaviour Therapy"
Jones, W. Paul
American Mental Health Counsellors Association Journal: Vol. 2., No. 2
(July 1980), pp. 53-58

This article indicates that improved physical appearance will frequently
improve both self-concept and the attainment of success.

"Education and the Living Image: Reflections on Imagery, Fantasy and
the Art of Recognition"
Abbs, Peter
Teachers' College Record, Vol. 82, No. 3 (Spring 1981) pp. 475-96

This article reveals the positive relationship between images and intellect.

Self Awareness Through the Creative Arts
Sanoff, Joan
May 1971, North Carolina Dept. of Labor

This article examines how a positive self-concept, developed through
creative arts, can be used to enhance one's career opportunities. Students
are shown as enrollees in New Careers Program which provides both
classroom and on-the-job training for the position of assistant teachers in
a pre-school. Enrollees are taken from the low income/minimal education
strata and it is their career aspirations that are being positively modified
through exposure to a variety of art forms.

Success Imagery for Young People
Holland, Margaret and Strickland, Alison

This kit provides two audio-cassettes with specific activities using imagery
and a report of a research study carried out with students in Florida.
    Results of the study indicated that students exposed to imagery on a
regular basis saw themselves as successful and showed an overall enhancement of self-concept.

"Self-Attitude Enhancement Through Positive Mental Imagery"
Patrizi, Frederic M.
Paper Presented at the Annual Convention of American Psychological
Association, August 1982

A study which examines the enhancement of self-attitude through the use
of positive mental imagery. Testing was done with the undergraduate
students. Half of the group was instructed in relaxation techniques prior
to the exposure to imagery sessions. Students then completed the Tennessee
Self-Concept Scale, the Zosenberg Self-Esteem Scale, and a revised Fish-
bein and Ajzen-type Scale of Self-Attitude. Only the latter test showed a
positive correlation between self-attitude and positive imagery.

"Modification of Locus Control: Using the RSI Technique in the Schools"
Stanton, H. E.
Contemporary Education Psychology, Vol. 7, No. 2 (April 1982), pp. 190-194

Relaxation suggestion and imagery (RSI) procedures were used to produce
greater internal control than that produced in a control group which
discussed ways of modifying locus of control.

"Creativity, General Systems and the Gifted"
Khatena, Joe
Gifted Child Quarterly, Vol. 23, No. 4 (Winter 1979), pp. 698-715

The theories of G. Land, J. Gowan, and J. Eccles are discussed in relation
to creative imagination, incubation, and right brain activity, all components of the General Systems approach.

The Mind's Eye
Sommer, Robert
1978 — Dell Publishing Co.

This book provides a theoretical look at the visualization process. Different
types of images and imagers are discussed with the inclusion of specific
examples and case studies. Text also includes questionnaires of assessing
visual imagery and an explanation of "The 3-D test for visualization skill."
The use of imagery and fantasy therapy is discussed. The author outlines
the values of imagery in human terms and notes its usefulness in many
aspects of the school experience.

Suggested Readings

Bry, Adelaide. *Visualization: Directing the Movies of Your Mind.* New York:
    Barns and Noble Books, 1979.

Clark, Barbara. *Growing Up Gifted.* Toronto: Charles E. Merrill Publishing Co., 1983.

Eberle, Bob. *Visual Thinking.* East Aurora, N.Y.: DOK, 1982, *Scamper Games for Imaginative Development.* East Aurora, N.Y.: DOK Pubs., 1977.

Ferguson, Marilyn. *The Aquarian Conspiracy–Personal and Social Transformation in the 1980's.* Los Angeles: J. P. Tarcher, Inc., 1980.

Fugitt, Eva D. *He Hit Me Back First.* Jalmar Press, California, 1983.

Galyean, Bev. *The Brain, Intelligence and Education; Implications for Gifted Programmes* (Roeper Review, Fall 1981).

———. *Language from Within.* Ken Zel Consultant Services, 767 Gladys Ave., Long Beach, CA. 90804, March 1976.

———. *Integrative Learning.* Ken Zel Consultant Services, 767 Gladys Ave., Long Beach, CA. 90804, 1980.

Hendrick, Gay, and Wills, Russel. *The Centering Book.* Englewood Cliffs, N.J.: Prentice-Hall, 1975.

Holland, Margaret, and Strickland, Alison. *Making Movies in Your Mind.* Applied Creative Learning Systems, 1982.

Holland, Margaret, and Strickland, Alison. *Success Imagery for Young People.* Applied Creative Learning Systems, 1982.

Kauffman, Draper L., Jr., *Teaching the Future. A Guide to Future-Oriented Education.* Palm Springs, California: ETC Publications, 1976.

Khatena, Joe. *Creative Imagination Imagery Actionbook.* Allan Associates Inc., Starkville, Mississippi.

———. *The Creatively Gifted Child.* Allan Associates Inc., Starkville, Mississippi.

———. *Teaching Gifted Children to Use Creative Imagination Imagery.* Allan Associates Inc., Starkville, Mississippi.

Lawrence, Jodi. *Alpha Brain Waves.* Los Angeles: Nash Pub., 1972.

Miller, John. *The Compassionate Teacher.* Englewood Cliffs, N.J.: Prentice-Hall, 1981.

Parnes, Sideny J., *The magic of your mind.* Buffalo, New York: Creative Education Foundation, Inc., 1981.

Parnes, Sidney J.; Noller, Ruth B.; Biondi, Angelo M., *Guide to Creative Action.* New York: Charles Scribner's Sons, 1977.

Plum, Lorraine. *Visual Thinking: A Whole-Brain Approach* (Challenge, March 1982).

Rowan, Roy. *The Intuitive Manager.* Toronto: Little, Brown and Company, 1986.

Sanders, Donald A., Sanders, Judith A. *Teaching Creativity through Metaphor.* New York: Longman Inc., 1984.

Seyba, Mary E. *Imagery: A Different Way of Thinking* (Educational Impressions, 1984).

Sommer, Robert. *The Mind's Eye.* New York: Dell Publishing Co., 1978.

Virship, Evelyn. *Right Brain People in a Left Brain World.* The Guild of Tutors Press, 1019 Gayly Ave., Los Angeles, California.

Whaley, Charles E. *Futures Studies: Personal and Global Possibilities.* New York: Trillium Press, 1984.

7

The Gifted Child in the World of Short Stories

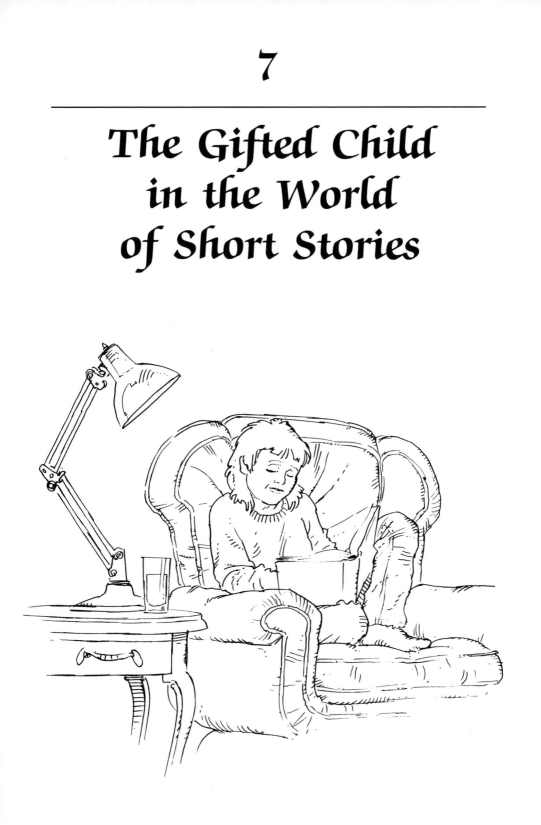

Introduction

The short story as a literary form has always been an important component in the development of a child's reading habits. Presenting the gifted child with a series of short stories which delineate traits of gifted behavior is simply an extension of this traditional practice.

Throughout the preceding sections of this book the authors have presented various ideas which are designed to assist the affective development of the gifted learner. The following collection of short stories sketch portraits of students who have thrived under the educational system and conversely individuals who are underachieving within the confines of the same system. Many of the situations which are depicted in this section of the book are based upon the author's experience in the teaching and learning situation.

The short stories are grouped so that readers may focus upon related issues, gifted education, and at the same time appreciate the attributes of gifted children. "Choices" and "The Longest Campaign," the first stories presented, deal with positive aspects of giftedness. Each of the main characters in these stories is a confident adolescent who displays high degrees of sensitivity and altruism which are frequently traits of the gifted learner. "Music and the Savage Beast" and "Summer Lessons" are examples of giftedness displayed in a non-academic setting. Generally it is hoped that such a setting influences the individual's social interaction, and enables the same person to perceive and relate better to the world around them. As well as perception, organizational abilities and shrewdness are other skills that are greatly appreciated in the adult world. When we examine a successful person's life we often wonder whether such ability was inherent or acquired? "A Short Lesson in Economics," "The Best of Plans," "Anson," and "Withdrawn" comprise the final group of stories and provide examples of the problems that may sometimes undermine the academic and social progress of the gifted child.

Some obstacles are created by the individual's unyielding nature, a trait that has been attributed to gifted students. Other impediments are created by the teacher who may be overburdened with pressing matters related to the needs of the group as a whole.

In addition to studying each of the short stories, the reader may wish to try some of the related activities. These are not merely exercises in reading comprehension; rather they are activities of a more independent and creative nature. Many of the short stories involve issues that are relevant to the shaping and functioning of our society. These activities — which promote discussion, research, thinking, and problem-solving — are intended to facilitate the moral and social development of the gifted student.

Matrix for Stories and Traits

The following scheme depicts the issues and qualities of giftedness found in each of the short stories:

Title	Issues/Qualities
Choices	sensitivity, courage
The Longest Campaign	altruism, determination, student government
Music and the Savage Beast	escapism, perception
Summer Lessons	empathy, autonomy
A Short Lesson in Economics	inventiveness, shrewdness
The Best of Plans	altruism, organization
Anson	inventiveness
Withdrawn	isolation, loneliness, program delivery

Choices

> **Purpose:** **Essentially a story of courage. Gifted children recognize the wide spectrum of their abilities but realize that in the final analysis they must take responsibility for their own decisions.**

"You have two choices in life: you can dissolve in the main stream, or you can be distinct. To be distinct, you may have to be different.
Alan Ashley Pitt

The students sat rigidly like birds who'd momentarily come to rest on a telephone wire. Their eyes focused straight ahead, almost unblinking, and their arms were extended, poised above a small, metallic buzzer. Seated opposite the eight students was a smartly dressed woman, who had reached for a card and was beginning to read in a voice that was both crisp and commanding.

"In what novel would you find the following characters: Scout, Dill and Atticus Finch?"

Almost immediately a buzzer flashed and a low, squawking noise echoed throughout the classroom.

"Mike?"

"To Kill a Mockingbird," came the reply.

"Correct. Ten points for Team B." She glanced at the clock. "Well that should do it as I believe twenty-five minutes have elapsed."

Placing the green cards in a small filing box she turned and looked at the portable scoreboard which had been operated by a student.

"Well, I see that for the second time in a row Team B has won. You people should be quite happy with yourselves," she said, pointing in the direction of Team B. However she was less effusive in her praise of the team that was seated to the left of her. "It appears that you people had better get to the library and brush up on your facts."

The members of Team A nodded their heads and made their exit from the room.

"Don't forget tomorrow's practice at 3:30," she called after them.

The remaining students began to gather up their jackets and books and moved toward the doorway.

"Mike, may I speak with you for a moment?"

A tall, broad-shouldered boy scooped up his hockey jacket and strode towards the teacher's desk.

"Yes, Mrs. Conroy?"

"Your team did quite well today. You've had a very good influence on them since you started attending practice on a regular basis."

The young boy smiled, revealing two front teeth that had temporarily been capped. "Typical Mrs. Conroy," he thought, "the iron fist in the velvet glove." Throughout Marshall Junior High School, the English teacher was appreciated for the firm, yet fair manner in which she conducted her classes.

"Thanks," said Mike, making apologetic gestures with his hands, "but I told you when I was chosen for the Quiz Kids that I couldn't make every practice because of my hockey commitments."

Mrs. Conroy rose from the desk and retrieved her briefcase from its resting place on top of the filing cabinet.

"You realize," she began, "that the next Quiz Kids game is on Monday. That leaves us with only two more days to practice. Now if you assure me that you will attend both sessions, I'll seriously consider playing you on Monday."

She crammed some test papers into her briefcase and closed it firmly. "It's up to you, Mike," she said.

Mike recognized the solemn tone of voice. No longer smiling, he reached for his books. "I'll see what I can do Mrs. Conroy. Goodnight." He walked down the long corridor no longer feeling elated about this afternoon's proceedings.

Walking home Mike tried to make some sense of the events of the day. Why is it, he thought, that whenever something wonderful happens something else happens which threatens to erase my good feelings? Here he was about to lose his chance to be a member of the Quiz Kids, an activity which he found both challenging and self-satisfying. It was him against the game itself. Having spent many years in team sports and group activities forced upon him by teachers he relished this academic one-to-one. Unlike the other members of the Quiz Kids team, he did not care about the potential T.V. appearance, a luxury awarded to the winning team members. No, the game itself was all the reward he needed.

Crossing the street he kicked a pop can and watched it first rebound off the curb and then lie dormant on the pavement. If only he could make his father understand his feelings about this new discovery in his life. Turning up the driveway that led to his house he was greeted by his father who was removing some cardboard boxes from the family car.

"Hi Mike."

"Hi Dad."

"Here son, give me a hand with these boxes," he said, handing some to Mike. "It looks as if your mother's about to get a head start on spring cleaning."

Together they went inside and placed the boxes in a corner of the basement.

After supper Mike mentioned his meeting with Mrs. Conroy and how she'd placed extra demands on his time. His father stiffened in his chair.

"You told her that you play hockey three nights a week, I assume."

Mike paused. "Kind of."

A distressed look appeared on his father's face.

"I said I'd see what I could do."

The older man toyed with his teacup, somewhat annoyed at the hesitancy in his son's voice. "Now look Mike, this team you're trying to make is this city's best Bantam club. Both Billy and Darren played on the Aeros and look how it turned out for them."

Just the mention of his older sons' names made his father's face take on a triumphant glow. Neither of Mike's older brothers were living at home and at last word both appeared on the verge of breaking into the N.H.L. "Now," continued his father, "if it worked for them, the Aeros should be good enough for you."

In the face of such persistence Mike felt his confidence ebbing, but still he went on.

"Why couldn't I stay with the Flyers as it's closer to home and the Flyers don't play as often as the other team. Then I could have more time for school activities. Besides if I don't make the Aeros, what then?" His father looked away in disgust.

"I knew we've been too soft with you, but I never expected this."

Mike felt stung by his father's inability to grasp the problem and said nothing.

"If you want a professional hockey career you'll have to make up your mind pretty quickly," said his father pushing his chair away from the table.

"Remember there's no room in the world for indecision." He tapped his forehead. "Mental toughness — it's everything."

Sitting there, alone in the kitchen, Mike sighed in despair. His worst imagined fears were now a reality. A decision would have to be made and soon. Tomorrow night Mike had a hockey practice at the same time as Mrs. Conroy expected him at the Quiz Kids practice. For the remainder of the evening Mike mulled the problem over in his mind and eventually he drifted into slumber, still undecided.

The following morning Mike was wandering through the school's hallways, still greatly preoccupied when he felt a tap on his shoulder. He turned and was surprised to see Mrs. Conroy.

"Good morning, Mike. I trust you haven't forgotten about tonight."

"Oh sure . . . Uh . . . Mrs. Conroy could I talk with you for a few minutes?"

"Sure," she said, recognizing his serious tone, "Why don't you walk with me to my next class?"

"Fine," he agreed, and fell in step with her.

As they walked, Mike related the details of his problem. After he had finished they continued to walk, neither person speaking. Mrs. Conroy finally broke the silence.

"Well it certainly is a complex issue. What will happen if you miss tonight's hockey practice?"

"I'll probably be cut from the team," he answered.

"Well aren't there other hockey teams you could play for? After all, this is a big city."

Mike stopped to hold the door for two students who were carrying a project table and then caught up with the teacher.

"This team means a great deal to my father. It's kind of a family thing."

"Well here we are Mike. I'm in this class next period." She reached into her purse and withdrew a set of keys. "What does this hockey team mean to you?"

Mike shifted his books from one hand to the other. "I guess that's what I'm trying to figure out Mrs. Conroy," he said in a very even voice.

She opened the door and paused for a moment. "Before you go to your next class there's something I'd like to leave with you.'' Mike watched her disappear inside the classroom. Somewhere inside of him he'd hoped that this decision would be removed from his hands, but he now realized that the decision was his alone. Just talking with Mrs. Conroy made him realize that any other action would be wrong.

''Step in for a minute.''

The teacher was at the front of the room flipping through the pages of a leather-bound book. ''Here we are.'' Taking a marker from her desk she placed it inside the book and after closing it, she handed the book to him. ''Read this poem, Mike. It won't make your decision for you, but I think it will let you see that there is something positive in what you're experiencing.''

Taking the book, he expressed his thanks to Mrs. Conroy and then proceeded out of the classroom and down the corridor to his next class. After exchanging greetings with some classmates Mike took his seat at the back of the room. Once the lesson had begun he reached for the book that Mrs. Conroy had given him and placed it inside his already opened Geography text. Turning to the page that she'd marked he saw it was a poem by Robert Frost, entitled, ''The Road Not Taken.'' Slowly he read it again marvelling at both the words on the page and Mrs. Conroy's intuitive powers.

With mixed feelings Mike finally closed the book. It'd be difficult to tell his father that he wouldn't be playing hockey with the Aeros. He wondered how his decision would affect their relationship which, as of late, was somewhat strained. And yet at the same time his apprehension was tempered by the present excitement he felt reading Frost's poem. For like the traveller, he too was about to embark upon the less-trodden but hopefully more challenging road.

Suggested Activities

1. Explain Pitt's quotation using examples from the life of someone you know.
2. Read ''The Road Not Taken.'' Research the life of Robert Frost. How has he taken the less-travelled road?
3. Write the conversation between Mike and his father, when Mike informs his Dad of his decision.
4. Write a ''Dear Abby'' style letter from Mike in which he outlines his dilemma. Also write the response from Abby to Mike.
5. Canadian universities, unlike their American counterparts, are not allowed to grant athletic scholarships. Research this issue and develop your point of view on the matter.

The Longest Campaign

> **Purpose:** **The character of Cathy Petrovic is used to illustrate the determination and ethical sense that are characteristics of gifted children.**

Cathy's eyes widened and the muscles in her face began to tighten. Surely Miss Holmes was kidding, or as the matronly home economics teacher was fond of saying, "having sport with them." Sitting opposite Cathy was Sandra Dinelli and it was clear that she too was astonished at the teacher's comments.

"So you can see girls, that such things as cooking and sewing are key elements in your lives." She paused momentarily to wipe her hands on a nearby towel and the girls noticed that when she resumed speaking, Miss Holmes' eyes had taken on a faraway look. "Yes, men admire an efficient housekeeper. They surely do."

The sharp blast of the school buzzer suddenly intruded upon Miss Holmes' homily. With a wave of her hand the class was dismissed amidst the clatter of slamming doors and the scraping of chairs upon tiled floors. Cathy and Sandra were the last of the thirty-four grade 8 girls to leave the home economics room and as they made their way down the hallway the two friends continued to discuss what they felt were Miss Holmes' antiquated comments.

"Do you believe that nonsense," said Cathy. "She's still living in the dark ages."

Sandra pointed toward one of the orange colored posters which adorned the school's hallway. "What would Miss Holmes think of that?" she asked in a dramatic tone of voice.

Cathy looked thoughtful for a moment. "Well, knowing Miss Holmes, she'd probably say that any girl who attempts to be student council president of *this* school is simply wasting her time."

Still acting, Sandra jumped in front of Cathy and placed both of her hands on Cathy's slim shoulders. "Cathy Petrovic," she began using her best Miss Holmes voice, "come to your senses and start behaving like the smart girl that I know you are. Let that nice boy, Brad Fulton, become student president. Who knows, he may even let you be this year's Winter Carnival Snow Queen!"

Cathy swooned and pressed the back of her hand to her forehead. "Oh yes, Miss Holmes, I'd do anything to be Bradley's snow queen." Both girls snorted with laughter.

"Hurry up Cath," said Sandra, still chuckling, "or we'll be late for History class."

Upon arriving in Room 115 they found Mr. Salter at the front of the class, eyeing empty seats and making the appropriate notations in his record. Quickly the girls headed towards their seats.

"Okay gang," he began, without discussion, "let's pick up from yesterday's class." From the top of his desk he chose a large silk-screened illustration in which a group of men from a prior era were seated around an oblong table.

"Now, who recognizes this famous gathering?"

"This year's staff photo!" interjected a voice. The class and Mr. Salter both laughed aloud.

"No, not quite . . . Yes, Brad?"

"The Fathers of Confederation."

Mr. Salter nodded and placed the print upon the ledge of the chalkboard. "Thank you, Brad. Now for the past month we've examined the facts which propelled us toward this historic occasion, so for the next little while we'll look at the players, the men who brought about this union of the colonies."

As the teacher spoke, Cathy stared at the illustration of the Fathers of Confederation. Something about it puzzled her, so she raised her hand.

"Sir," she asked with great seriousness, "why were there no women present at the Conferences in Charlottetown and Quebec?"

"That's a very complicated question, and I might add, one we will examine in the final term when we study women's rights. Put simply enough Cathy, women in the 1860s were not a dominant social force as instead they tended to be more concerned with domestic chores."

The teacher's final words prompted a great deal of snickering from the boys, prompting Brad to voice his opinion.

"They were absolutely right," he said, gesturing at the Fathers of Confederation. "Politics is a man's world."

"Hear! Hear!" chorused a few boys as if they were parliamentarians.

"What's wrong Brad! You're not afraid of a little competition, are you?" inquired Cathy, to the hoots of the few girls who were in the class.

Quickly, Mr. Salter intervened. "Okay, that's enough of that nonsense." He turned to face Brad, who was seated at the far side of the room. "I suggest you save your quips for tomorrow's assembly. And as for you, Cathy, since you're so concerned about the plight of women in the 1860s, maybe you could research the topic and enlighten the class by reporting to us. Agreed?"

Reluctantly Cathy nodded her head and the History class continued without any further interruptions.

After class Sandra and Cathy went to the cafeteria where they were to meet Kent O'Connor, one of the few boys who'd volunteered to help with Cathy's campaign. They found him seated near the large windows which bordered one side of the lunchroom.

"Hi Kent. It looks as though I'll have to pass on today's strategy meeting. Salter's given me a research assignment for tomorrow."

Kent nodded at Cathy, unable to reply as his mouth was full of potato chips.

"Nice manners, Kent," she said laughingly. "Sandra see what the chip king here has come up with and I'll call you tonight so we can discuss tomorrow's assembly."

"Sure thing," replied Sandra, seating herself across from Kent. "Good luck with the research." "Thanks," said Cathy, trying to sound enthusiastic.

Later that night after completing her homework Cathy grabbed her blue binder, which the kids in her campaign group jokingly called The Manifesto, and went to telephone Sandra.

"Hi Sandra."

"Hi Cath. How'd it go with the research?"

"Great. Salter will flip when he sees the facts that I dug up. It's too bad we couldn't zap Brad and his gang back to the year 1867. They'd love it. Women couldn't vote, they were legally beaten by their husbands and they couldn't attend university. In fact it was so strict that one lady disguised herself as a man so she could attend medical school in Toronto." Cathy heard a low whistle at the other end of the telephone line.

"Yes, we've certainly come a long way," said Sandra mockingly.

"Okay, let's get serious for a moment, shall we? What did Kent have to say?" inquired Cathy.

"Not a heckuva lot," replied Sandra. "It seems that Brad is still only going after the boys' votes, with his macho-man-for-president line."

Upon hearing this, a worried look crossed Cathy's face. Glancing at the papers in front of her she began to recite some figures to Sandra.

"Let's see. We have 860 eligible voters. Of that number there are 511 boys and 349 girls." She paused briefly, reflecting upon her own statement and continued. "I really think we should bring Mr. Chauvinist Pig out into the open and show the students how narrow his views are."

"It's a little late for changes, Cath. Besides I think you have to give the boys some credit. Not every guy in the school believes that males are superior to females. They might say that to be part of the group but voting is done secretly so that's in our favor." She paused to catch her breath. When Sandra was serious she could be quite convincing. "The kids know you're a good student, Cathy. You have respect, especially after the Christmas Cheer Campaign you ran last year."

"So what you're saying is we shouldn't lower ourselves to Brad's level."

"Exactly," replied Sandra. "Let's stick to our guns and keep hitting them with the issues."

Listening to such advice made Cathy feel good. She and Sandra had known each other for years and it was Sandra who'd encouraged her to end the male domination of the school's student council. Smiling, Cathy gathered a sheaf of papers in her hand and spoke into the mouthpiece of the telephone.

"Okay if I read my speech?"

In a clear and confident voice Cathy read through her well written speech in which she outlined the type of junior high school community that her student council would attempt to create. When she had finished she heard Sandra applauding on the other end of the line. "You've got my vote, Cathy."

"Great. Four hundred and thirty more and we'll be in. Well I better get going. I'm starting to get some dark glances from my father. See you tomorrow."

"See you," said Sandra.

For the remainder of the night Cathy stood in front of the mirror practising her speech imagining an attentive crowd within the silver rimmed glass. Needless to say she finished her speech to wild imaginary applause. The one snicker was courtesy of her younger brother, who'd crept into the room undetected. After one more run-through Cathy decided to call it a night. She knew she'd need a good sleep in order to keep her wits about her tomorrow.

The following day Cathy was backstage, pacing and glancing at her speech, which she'd printed on small cream-colored file cards. Peering through a gap in the stage curtains, she could see the students filing noisily into the school auditorium. Normally assemblies offered nothing more than a break from daily classes. However this head-on confrontation between members of the opposite sex had aroused some electoral interest in the student body. Yes indeed, from a student's point of view, today's political forum promised to be entertaining, especially if Brad Fulton began "baiting" Cathy Petrovic as he'd boasted he would do.

"Well Petrovic, all set to be put in place!"

Instantly Cathy recognized the sneering voice. "If you mean student council president, then yes I'm all set to be put in my place." She looked at him triumphantly.

"Trust me Petrovic , there's not a guy out there who'll vote for you," he said, waving wildly toward the curtain.

"What a jerk," thought Cathy. However she kept her temper in check and tried to turn the tables on him. "Memorized your speech yet, Brad? I'm sure it must have taken all of 30 seconds."

Brad stared at her and his eyes narrowed as he too fought to control his rising anger. "You're really very amusing Petrovic. I'll remember that at Winter Carnival time." Walking away he turned to face her and then delivered the punch line, "Yes, this year you could be Carnival Clown!" he hissed, and then laughed heartily at his own joke.

"Well I see you're quite relaxed Brad," remarked Mr. Salter, emerging from the shadows.

"All set to win, sir," he replied.

The old teacher eyed Brad with a bored expression. "Well let's get on with it." He then made a motion at one of the students acting as a stagehand to draw back the curtains.

Watching the two pieces of blue cloth separate, Cathy scanned the audience, looking for reassuring faces. Seated directly in front of the stage, some twenty rows away, were Sandra and Kent. Together they gave her the thumbs-up sign.

"Good morning," began Mr. Salter. "The format of today's electoral assembly will be as follows. Each candidate will be given five minutes in which to deliver a speech and then in the remaining time, members of the audience may question the candidates. Obviously such questions will only deal with the student council election and not personal issues. Those who choose to do otherwise will find themselves sitting on the office bench."

Muffled laughter and mumbled obscenities drifted through the auditorium. Cathy, having won the toss of the coin, had chosen to speak first sensing that the attention span of her peers would be rather short. Positioning herself behind the microphone and palming her cue cards, she launched into her speech. The students, impressed with her crisp, certain delivery gave her an enthusiastic round of applause when she finished speaking. Furthermore she'd managed to convey her passionate belief that the school needed students who were positive and socially aware. As expected, Brad Fulton's speech was short on substance and long on chauvinist rhetoric. He had the largely male crowd constantly chuckling at his gentle swipes at womanhood and, not surprisingly, he too received a warm round of applause.

However, once the audience took over the forum, Brad's role was greatly reduced as students began to query Cathy concerning her plans for increasing school spirit and other related issues. Frantically, some of Brad's campaign workers began asking questions of their candidate, thus allowing him to exercise his considerable penchant for put-downs. As a result, the assembly closed on a more even note than it had begun, much to Cathy's dismay. She leaned forward in her chair, trying to look interested in Mr. Salter's final words.

"... Finally, I'd just like to remind you people that voting takes place during the lunch hours and the winner will be announced during today's last period. You should now proceed to your period three classes."

Backstage Mr. Salter commended both students for having run good campaigns. After Brad had walked away with some friends and was out of earshot, the teacher addressed Cathy, who was not doing a good job hiding her disappointment at the turn of events in the assembly.

"I'm proud of the way you conducted yourself through this thing, Cathy. Sometimes keeping one's dignity is a very difficult thing to do, especially in politics."

She thanked him for his sincere interest and left the auditorium wondering if the rest of the school would be as objective as was Mr. Salter.

During the seventh period she received an answer to that question, from Mrs. Totten, the school's vice-principal.

"Excuse me teachers for this interruption but I've been asked to announce the results of today's student council election."

Cathy placed her hands on top of the desk and waited for the announcement to continue.

"Eligible voters — 860, students absent — 15, spoiled — 4. Therefore a total of 841 votes were cast." Again the voice halted, as if figures were still to be double-checked. Cathy folded her hands waiting.

"Brad Fulton — 431 votes, Cathy Petrovic — 410 votes. The new school president is Brad Fulton. Once again, my thanks to Mr. Salter and all those who took part in this year's election."

There was a click in the P.A. speaker as Mrs. Totten signed off. Whoops of joy were heard reverberating throughout the corridor of the second floor hallway. Cathy stared at her desk, feeling as if someone had squeezed the breath out of her. It was as if a great wave of fatigue had enveloped her. Cautiously, Sandra approached her desk.

"I'm sorry Cath. We did everything we could." Her voice was reassuring and for the second time in the last few days Cathy was struck by the value of her friendship.

"Thanks, Sandra."

A second person appeared at Cathy's desk.

"Look at these totals," said Kent, waving a piece of paper. "Cathy, you convinced close to 100 of the guys that you'd make a better president than Brad. I'd say that's progress."

"Who was it," said Sandra, "who said we may have lost the battle, but we'll win the war?"

"Nellie McClung maybe," answered Cathy with a small smile. Her friends looked at her puzzled and Cathy thought to herself, what would the great emancipator have said about my campaign? She'd probably congratulate me, she replied in answer to her own question, for not disguising myself. And to Cathy, that was what really mattered.

Activities

1. Any type of research assignment; that is, women's rights, discrimination.
2. Does your school have student government? If so, what kind? What are the pertinent issues? If your school does not have student government, design one.
3. Using their points of view, write Cathy's or Brad's speech incorporating topical issues.
4. Dramatize a scene in which Cathy confronts Miss Holmes.
5. How would Canadian history have been different if our first Prime Minister had been a woman?

Summer Lessons

> **Purpose:** The relationship between an apparently selfish boy and two senior citizens is outlined. Once again the gifted child is shown as keenly empathetic, as well as capable of existing on a highly independent level.

Down on my belly, oblivious to the dampness that was soaking my clothing, I slithered along the ground like some purposeful reptile. My heart, fully aware of the lessons of combat, hammered the earth beneath my chest. Straining my neck, I lifted my eyes skyward and scanned the horizon for the sight of my pursuers. A sigh, barely audible, passed through my lips. Leaping to my feet, I sprinted along the broadside of a hill until a large, billowing oak tree was reached. Crouching behind the tree, I gulped some air and then roughly wiped my face with a soiled headband. Taking further advantage of this momentary lull in the action, I mentally reviewed my assignment. H. G. had instructed me to intrude upon enemy territory, skirt the perimeter of their rear flank, and then detect a weakness in their key holding compound. Still pondering my next move, I suddenly heard the collective roar of human voices, some 500 metres to the south of me. Cautiously I stepped out from behind the tree. Our flag had been captured! The screeching blast of a whistle confirmed my observation and reluctantly I began to make my way back to the meeting place.

Walking through the silent forest I gradually became aware of the fact that the fun part of my summer holiday was now over. For the past two weeks I'd been erratically darting about the campgrounds, trying to stretch my stay here into an eternity. Silverhills Camp had that kind of effect on kids. You arrived here full of homesickness and spent the first day listening to a million rules delivered by some Rocky lookalike. However, a few games and outings later you stopped counting the days until the bus left for home. Simply enough, you were hooked on Silverhills.

''Good game guys. I guess the Chiefs will have to even the score next year. Now, hand your headbands to either Ted or me, and then get your gear and meet by the playground.''

With one last burst of joyous energy, we campers sprinted to our cabins. A thousand goodbyes later I was aboard the bus heading back to the city. Most of the other kids were seated in small groups, chatting and exchanging addresses. Others debated over who'd really deserved to win the game of capture-the-flag. I knew I'd never be back at Silverhills. Silently I stared out the window watching blurred landscapes, and filing the experiences of the past two weeks in the good memories compartment of my brain. That was what I like best about pleasant memories, the fact that on a lazy, Saturday afternoon or a boring school day you could simply dig through your mental file and constantly chase away the blues. Somehow during the next two weeks, I was certain that I'd be reaching into my file quite often.

Riding the bus I began to rethink the deal that I'd struck with my parents. However, in order to fully comprehend this particular deal, you'll have to meet my family, so bear with me for a moment.

My father is an account executive with a large advertising firm and from all reports is very good at his job. For example, he recently was given an all-expense paid holiday to Europe which he delayed until the summer so that he and my mother could celebrate their twenty-fifth wedding anniversary overseas. He's also a romantic kind of guy so naturally this was to be a "no-kids allowed" holiday. The unfair part was that I was shipped east for a month as Mom and Dad reasoned that my three sisters, all of whom are married, had enough responsibility without dumping me on them. Besides, they said, it's time I expanded my cultural horizons, and you don't argue with that kind of logic. So, I was allowed to choose a summer camp for two weeks and was then to spend two more weeks with my grandmother in Toronto. My mother felt that I'd be good company for her mother, who lived alone. Looking beyond the obvious, I figured that my trip east was the result of my parent's guilt since this was the first summer in which they wouldn't be making the annual pilgrimage to visit her in Toronto.

Looking out the front window of the bus I could see the skyline of the city in the distance. A maze of green and blue signs informed me that we were travelling upon Highway 400 and that the great city was only thirty kilometres away. Slouching back in my seat I silently cursed my fate and wondered what I would do for the next two weeks. I hoped Grandma had cable television.

After what seemed like a very short drive, the bus eased into some place called the York Mills Kiss'n Ride Station. Crazy thoughts danced in my mind as the bus driver, whom I thought looked a little weird, handed me my luggage from the storage compartment. Mumbling thanks, I scurried away into the subway station only to be pounced upon by my grandmother, who promptly kissed me on the cheek.

"Kristopher, you get taller every time I see you."

"Hi Grandma," I replied, while automatically wiping away her kiss, praying that there were no lipstick smudges on my face.

She reached for my suitcase.

"It's okay, I can manage."

She chuckled. "I keep forgetting that you're now twelve years old! Well we'd better find the car," she said, steering me towards the parking lot. I imagined that the car was in the Primp'n Park, but upon finding the small, blue Chevrolet I noticed nothing of the sort. Wearily I plopped my suitcase in the back seat of the car. Throughout the drive to her house, Grandma quizzed me about my family's current adventures. Seeing as I was somewhat of a stand-in for my parents I did my best to be evasive. However, I was no match for the practised double speak of my parents and by the end of our fifteen-minute ride, the old fox had thoroughly interrogated me. Once again I manfully lugged my suitcase, and was told to place it in one of the spare bedrooms. Looking about the small room I sensed that for the next two weeks this would be my sanctuary.

During supper Grandma continued to quiz me from a repertoire of questions that seemed inexhaustible. I'd once mentioned this to my sister by noting that Grandma was somewhat "nosey". Expecting to be commended for my insight, I was instead rebuked. My sister quickly pointed out that

Grandpa had only been dead for five years, and the older lady was still adjusting to the loneliness of her situation. Her keen interest in our family was because of love, not gossip. As she talked, I looked at the happiness on my grandmother's face and I began to sense that what I called a visit was for her an occasion. Recalling my condescending attitude toward her, I felt rather guilty, so when she asked if I'd like to go to the hospital with her I said okay.

While driving through the tree lined city streets she explained that this was not an ordinary hospital. Instead it was similar to a nursing home, only the occupants were all victims of the wars in which Canada had been involved. Grandma performed volunteer services at the hospital's library. It sounded like an uncomplicated job and in fact her most vital function was to provide the veterans with the feeling that somebody still cared.

"Over there on the right is Sunnybrook Hospital."

She carefully manoeuvred the car into a parking space. Looking to my right I saw a massive series of buildings. Many of them were fronted by smudged brick and rows of rectangular shaped windows, while a few other of the buildings were constructed of recently poured concrete. In front of each building was an undecorative black and white sign with an alphabetical letter affixed to it.

"We're heading in this direction," said Grandma, gesturing towards the newest of all the buildings. The tall, asbestos-colored structure was bordered by a park-like setting. At ground level, in front of the building, were men in wheelchairs, some of them with their legs covered by old tartan blankets, despite the warm weather. I'd always been taught never to stare, but the sight of a man with no legs propped in a wheelchair made my eyes bulge. The man's legs had been removed around the area of the middle thigh and now resembled someone's elbows, all round and pointed. Drifting past him, I overheard him and another verteran discussing his grandson's recent job promotion.

"Hurry up Kristopher, I'm almost late."

I quickened my pace and attempted to close the gap between Grandma and me. Despite her age she still moved like a newly purchased tennis ball. As she led me through the vast foyer, adorned by its high ceilings and photographic prints, I again encountered the men in wheelchairs. Some were clustered together playing cards and chatting noisily. Others stared silently through the expansive windows at the parklands which were adjacent to the hospital. A white-haired man with a gnarled face and ratty housecoat stared at me as if I'd intruded upon his home. Maybe I had. Or quite possibly it was my youth, my healthy limbs that startled him. Whatever, his intense gaze made me squirm so I continued to keep pace with my grandmother. When we'd reached the end of the foyer, we then headed down a narrow hallway to the hospital library.

The room was much smaller than any library I'd seen, but was amply stocked with books. A buffalo head hung from one of the walls reminding me of the perils of extinction.

"See the artwork on this bulletin board? It was done by the men and women who live in the hospital," informed my grandmother as she steered me towards a temporarily erected display board. Examining the work I noticed that many of the perspectives were from the inside of the hospital. Only someone forever confined to a hospital room could have drawn with such precise detailing. It struck me that even the most beautiful of places could be confining.

"Bonjour Doris."

I stepped away from the artwork and turned to face the owner of the accented voice.

"Well hello Andre."

"I'm 'ere for my story."

His name was Andre Duvet and like many of the men here in the hospital, he'd had his legs amputated. He also possessed a left arm that was withered with the same rounded edges as his legs. Dressed in a light colored shirt and drab khaki shorts he looked too frail to be the owner of such a commanding voice.

"Andre, I'd like you to meet my grandson, Kristopher. He's come all the way from Vancouver to visit with me."

Immediately the old man thrust out his good, right hand. Stepping toward him I shook hands, feeling my hand become lost in the old man's powerful grip.

"Nice to meet you, sir."

"Call me Andre," he replied, still holding my now throbbing hand.

"Okay." Finally he released my hand.

My grandmother then approached us armed with a chair and a novel.

"Usually I read to Andre, but maybe as a special treat you'd read to him today?" "Read to him?" I asked, somewhat confused. Then it suddenly occurred to me that maybe he'd been blinded in the war. However, the old veteran quickly removed such thoughts from my mind.

"I grew up in Northern K'bec. At 10 years I was working the asbestos mines. At 18 I signed up to fight. 21, I came here and have been here ever since."

The old man's grip on his chair tightened, but his eyes remained level with mine.

"Andre never learned to read," interjected my grandmother. She patted the old man on the shoulder. "No matter. We here at the library love to read to him." She reached for the paperback, but I beat her to it. She smiled and I sensed that I was being challenged, even though I didn't quite understand why. Gripping the book as if it were some medieval gauntlet, I wheeled Andre into a corner of the room and got myself down across from him. Leaning back in his wheelchair Andre closed his eyes and waited.

Apprehensively I eyed the title of the book, *All Quiet on the Western Front*. Strange I thought, a war veteran wanting to listen to a combat story. You'd think that he'd lived enough of real battles. Opening the novel I silently scanned the preface and it was then that the irony of this situation began to surface. The story, according to the preface, was about the men who despite outwitting death had their lives ruined forever by the war.

"Come on boy. Get on with it," commanded the quiet voice.

And so I did. Using my best read-to-class voice I stumbled through the opening pages of the novel. Occasionally I would mangle a German name only to be corrected by Andre. I sensed that he knew the story better than I. Indeed he did. After a half hour's reading Andre began to reminisce about his own war memories and soon the novel was discarded. He'd been injured in France in 1944 during the Allied invasion. His maiming involved no daring rescues nor great escapes. Instead he'd simply been cut in half by German gunfire while attempting to hold down a beach-head gunpost. As he spoke I thought of the war games that we'd played at camp and was embarrassed by the seriousness of them. After awhile Andre grew tired and a lady in a green smock came to take him back to his room. As he was leaving he offered his hand.

"Nice meeting you son. Maybe you'll come and read to me again, eh?"

"Yes sir. I'd like that."

The lady wheeled him out of the room and my eyes followed the old soldier, sitting so tall despite his fatigue. Suddenly I became aware of my grandmother's arm around my shoulders. Looking up at her I smiled knowing that my warm memories file had just become one file richer.

Suggested Activities

1. Visit some veterans or senior citizens and write about your visit seen through their eyes.
2. Read Erich Remarque's *All Quiet on the Western Front.*
3. Using news clippings, magazines, and so on, develop a personal stand on nuclear arms.
4. Research the Royal Canadian Legion or War Amputees Society and present a report to the class.
5. What are the non-physical injuries of war? Research the causes and related therapies of this problem.

A Short Lesson in Economics

> **Purpose:** **A different view of giftedness — the young entre-**
> **preneur who uses everyday activities as a way**
> **of coping with academic drudgery.**

I waited patiently for the priest and his procession to leave the altar. As he walked past our pew, he appeared to glance in my direction. Reflexively I began to lip-synch the response to "The Mass Has Ended." Appeased, the good Father looked away and headed for the rear of the church. Taking my proper cue, I began to wend my way down the aisle. Heading through the small foyer I made sure to obtain the weekly church bulletin. This was a ritual that had begun during childhood and now had simply become one more process in my ritualistic church-going behavior. After exchanging glazed looks with the bulletin issuer, I nodded "good day" at Father Brenchley and headed out into the sticky August midday heat.

Sitting in my car, I absently began to read this week's bulletin. More of the ritual. Always wait for five minutes in the parking lot, otherwise there's a good chance of being rear-ended by one of my "Christian brothers." One particular item in the newsletter caught my eye — Attention students, former staff and students of St. Raphael's, on Saturday, September 30th, the school will be holding its 25th Anniversary Reunion Dance.

I shook my head and laughed aloud. St. Raphael's! It had been close to twenty years but the memories of those days were still vivid. One particular character was even more recallable. In fact, one couldn't think of St. Raphael's and not remember K. C. Wentworth.

K. C. Wentworth — upon first glance he was just another grade 6 student. However, ten minutes of his company soon alerted even the dullest of souls to the fact that K. C. would never, ever be ordinary. His full name was Kenneth Clarence Wentworth, but early in his life some sympathetic relative had done him a great favor and labeled him K. C., and as far as we at St. Raphael's were concerned a guy couldn't ask for a better "handle."

He was, however, admired for more than his name. Teachers despised him and naturally this made him a hero in the eyes of his peers. K. C. would always correct the teacher's occasional lapses in spelling, but in a manner that commanded the attention of the whole class.

"Excuse me Mr. Downs, I hate to be fussy about this, but are you sure that 'accompany' is only spelled with one 'c'? The book that I was reading this morning had it printed with two 'c's'."

Poor old Mr. Downs would sputter and then yell for the dictionary. K. C. would lean back in his chair, confidently waiting for his certain triumph. When it occurred, and it always did, Mr. Downs would quietly head to the blackboard and make the appropriate correction, then glance in K. C.'s direction and apply the "stare." This meant one and only one thing — notebook check. Sure enough, old Mr. Downs would head down the aisle and snatch K. C.'s canary-colored notebook from his desk, inspect it, and then rave about the sloppy handwriting, the lack of a title, and the lines that were drawn without the use of a ruler. Such a scene was generally repeated biweekly and was welcome diversion from the daily drudgery.

Mr. Downs was not alone in his dislike of K. C. Our rotary subject teachers were also victims of his corrections and rebuttals. Their response was similar to Mr. Downs as they too lambasted his shoddy notes. However, after each test they simply shook their heads as K. C. consistently scored above the rest of the class. Needless to say, school for K. C. was a necessary evil. So in his own way, he decided to make the best of it. Yes, K. C. was the first real entrepreneur that I ever knew. Later in my adult life, I realized that this particular skill often bordered on larceny. Nevertheless, his antics were legendary.

Early in the school year, K. C. detected a serious deficiency in the lifestyle of the average eleven-year-old boy. The problem was money, or more aptly, the lack of it. Accordingly, he quickly developed a scheme which would remedy this malady and for some unexplained reason chose me as his accomplice.

We met one Saturday morning at the corner of Brinston and Lawrence and then headed to a destination of which only K. C. was certain. As we walked, he explained the situation.

"We're heading to the old age home. They're holding their annual fall fun fair and I thought we might lounge about and see if there's some loose change to be made."

My worst fears were confirmed! We were on a stealing mission! He recognized my apprehension.

"Don't worry Ace. This is on the up and up. Perfectly 'legit'."

It was times such as this when I thought K. C. had watched too many episodes of the "Untouchables". When we arrived at the old age home we found it brimming with activity. K. C. went right to work and began to wander purposefully amongst the clientele. Myself, I became absorbed in the balloon toss and in a matter of moments had squandered my weekly allowance, which was the princely sum of twenty-five cents.

A few moments later I caught sight of K. C., only now he was clutching a paper satchel to his chest. He gestured in my direction and I followed him.

"Where are we going?"

"To the store," came the confusing reply.

Once inside the I.G.A., K. C. went straight to the courtesy bar and dumped the bulging satchel upon the counter.

"Ten pop bottles."

The young girl behind the counter peeked inside the brown bag, rang the cash register, and handed K. C. two dimes.

"Thanks," he said, and headed toward the exit.

Following at his heel, I tried hard to contain my exuberance.

"Now what?" I asked.

"Back to the fun fair," came the reply. "We'll get another load of bottles and then cash them in here."

I whistled in appreciation of his scheme. However, I still had some reservations about the legality of the operation.

"Where exactly are you finding these pop bottles?"

"People drink their pop and then discard the empty bottle."

"But aren't the bottles the property of the fun fair people?"

"Sure they are," he replied. "Look Ace, we're doing them a big favor as we're keeping the grounds free of litter. Therefore, it's only fair that we extract a small fee for such a service."

"Sounds fair to me," I said, nodding my head.

"Sure it does," said K. C., and with that he darted across the street.

After what seemed like our tenth trip to the I.G.A., K. C. suggested that we call it a day.

"What!" I cried. "This is just the start of a very profitable day!"

He eyed me with what seemed a look of great severity.

"You can never be too greedy," he said solemnly.

For a brief moment I considered a solo operation, but quickly rejected such an enterprise. And so ended the great pop bottle scheme.

I immediately took my share of the profits and went on a small scale candy binge.

Not K. C. though. On Monday he showed up with his assorted change and placed it in an old Listerine throat lozenge case. Burying the case inside his cluttered desk, he then proceeded to go about the routines of the school day. It wasn't until lunch time that I began to realize the significance of the Listerine case. In those days most of my classmates stayed at school for lunch. Thus, fluids were a necessity if one were to choke down that dry bologna and mustard sandwich. For this reason our school sold orange juice and milk during the lunch hour period.

However, on this particular day, Kenny Cole had forgotten the all important drink money. K. C. was quick to realize Kenny's predicament.

"Say Kenny, how about I lend you the money?"

Kenny's eyes widened.

"Would you?"

"Sure thing. I'll give you a dime today and you pay me fifteen cents by Friday."

Kenny's eyes narrowed. Then he took a long hard look at the stack of sandwiches in front of him. He swallowed hard.

"It's a deal."

K. C. reached into his desk, removed the blue case, and carefully selected a dime from it. He then reached into his shirt pocket and removed a small scratch pad on which he made some illegible notations. Flipping the notebook shut, he smiled and handed Kenny the dime.

As the month wore on the class became witness to this routine many times over. And then one day the lending services stopped. Immediately I approached K. C. and inquired about it. Once again he gave me a look of impatience.

"Like I said before Ace, you can never be too greedy."

Indeed those very needs had become K. C.'s credo in all of his schemes, and yet I never truly appreciated the wisdom of this seemingly simple statement until the spring of our grade 6 year.

Sometime during the year, K. C. had acquired a paper route. The paper was a neighborhood tabloid which was delivered every Wednesday after school. At first K. C. was a top-notch paperboy and naturally enough even won some kind of circulation award. However, the novelty of the route quickly waned and K. C. was soon ready to unleash another scheme. For this enterprise K. C. employed the "Tom Sawyer" approach, as each Wednesday morning K. C. could be found at the back of the class extolling the many virtues of delivering papers. However, his impassioned appeal fell upon deaf ears. Realizing a desperate situation, K. C. then offered a quarter for each day's delivery. Such a generous offer struck a nerve and there were numerous volunteers for the job. He then began the selection process, making sure that no one did the route more than once. This was no doubt due to K. C.'s strong democratic beliefs.

The paper route enterprise ran quite smoothly until one of the volunteer paper boys requested his entitled payment. Such a request however did not fizz K. C.

"I have to collect from my customers before I can make any payments. Once this is done you boys will receive a full and satisfactory payment, most likely at the end of the month."

The month's end arrived and still no payments had been made. It appeared to me that K. C. had strayed from his staunch monetary beliefs. Needless to say the boys were quite upset and references were made to the dismantling of K. C.'s anatomy. It was with such a purpose in mind that the boys headed to K. C.'s house.

Upon arriving they found K. C. lounging on his front step.

"Hi guys. I was hoping you'd come by. I've got your payment and I'm sure you'll find it to your liking."

He went inside and he reappeared with a small brown carton.

"Now, I promised everyone a quarter. Correct?"

The five boys nodded their heads.

"Well guys," he began, eyeing the carton in his hands, "I don't think that money is an adequate means of expressing my thanks. No, instead I've decided to give each one of you a Lola."

A Lola was a terrifically refreshing ice flavored drink, which if eaten properly could provide thirty minutes of palatable pleasure. They also cost forty cents apiece. The boys were ecstatic. They quickly took their rewards and walked away chortling at how they had more than evened the score with K. C. Wentworth.

I stared at K. C. My confidence in his entrepreneurial abilities was visibly shaken. He simply watched the boys swagger up the street, then gave me a knowing wink, turned and went inside the house.

That night after supper my mother said we kids could have a treat.

"I was at the I.G.A. today and they had Lolas on sale, so I bought two boxes."

My spirits began to rise. I raced to the freezer and reached for the carton of Lolas. Sure enough, there it was in black and white — eight Lolas for one dollar and twenty cents. Amazing! Simply amazing!

The blast of a car horn jarred my dulled senses. Looking up, I realized that I was impeding the progress of a red Buick. Tossing the bulletin on the seat, I turned the ignition key and gunned the engine. Steering my car towards the exit, my thoughts began to drift back to St. Raphael's and the upcoming reunion. I made a mental note of attending and keeping an eye peeled for K. C. Knowing K. C., I'm sure he'll have the concession rights for name tags. I only hope that he lets me in on the action.

Suggested Activities

1. At what profession would K. C. excel? Why?
2. List the qualities needed for various professions. Design a situation where K. C. meets J. R. (for example, K. C. as encyclopedia salesperson meets J. R. the gambler).
3. Complete research on entrepreneurs. What is an entrepreneur? Give modern examples.
4. Every classroom needs a K. C. Write about the day he comes to your class.

The Best of Plans

> **Purpose:** An illustration of the altruistic child. Also shows the excellent leadership skills of the gifted learner.

"Hey Mitch! Go downstairs and get me these things, okay?"

A dark-haired boy appeared from behind the magazine rack and took the folded sheet of paper from the older man.

"Sure thing George," said Mitch, as he helped himself to a piece of green licorice. Munching contentedly, he ambled down the aisle towards the back of the store, and then disappeared down the steep staircase.

The old store owner shuffled in behind the counter and wearily plopped himself down on the wooden stool which was situated behind the well-worn NCR cash register. Adjusting the glasses on his nose, he studiously began to leaf through a packet of invoices. Exhaling deeply, he then made a note of each supplier — Dominion Dairies, Wrigley's Chewing Gum, Lowney's Candy Company, and so on. George Kovacs sadly shook his head and contemplated his fate. How could he pay these bills if he never had any customers?

"George! You're getting low on the family-size bottles of Coca Cola and Seven-Up."

Acknowledging the voice, the old man discarded his invoices and removed some of the cartons from the large pile in the boy's arms.

"Put them here Mitch and we'll unpack them."

"There's a few other things you should order," Mitch said, as he reached for the scratch pad. "Here, I'll write them down for you."

The old man grabbed his arm.

"I don't think I'll be placing any orders for a few weeks."

Mitch glanced at the store owner.

"C'mon George, you'd hate to run short on something. It'd be bad for business."

The older man tore a top off a box of Hershey bars.

"Nobody comes into Kovacs' Variety Store anymore. Instead they all go to that new 7-11 store with its hot sandwiches and fancy freeze drinks. No, the era of the neighborhood cigar store is coming to an end. The people, they want wide aisles, bright lights, and plenty of selection."

He gazed about his own dusty, overcrowded store and with a hint of pride in his voice said, "No, this certainly isn't a 7-11 store."

Mitch was listening intently to the words of George Kovacs. Such was the nature of their relationship. The kindly, old European befriended the boy two years ago and eventually gave him a job in the store. Mitch came to work everyday and usually helped out for three hours. He never received any money for his efforts, nor did he want any such rewards. Instead he was free to partake in all that the store had to offer. As well, Mitch received a worldly helping of the wisdom of George Kovacs. The store owner had given the boy books to read, he'd shown him how to play cribbage, and currently was instructing Mitch in the finer points of chess. Indeed,

Kovacs had been just like a father to Mitch, the father that Mitch had never known as he'd died when Mitch was four years old. Similarly, Kovacs knew what it was like to be alone since the death of his wife two years ago.

"George, do you remember that book you gave me to read last month, the one about the old man and his struggle with the sea?"

The eyes of the older man took on a faraway look.

"Yes, that was Hemingway — a great writer."

"Exactly. Now what did the old man do when the waves started to pound against his tiny boat and his hands bled from the exertion of hanging onto the fishing line? Did he give up?"

"You're a good boy Mitch, but this store is no sea and me, I'm no fisherman."

He paused and gestured towards the front of the store.

"It is the customers who will determine the fate of this store."

For the remainder of the day the two friends were silent. However, as Mitch said good-night to George, he silently promised himself that he would find a solution to the store owner's dilemma.

The following day, Mitch dropped by the store to tell George that he wouldn't be coming by for the next couple of days as he had some pressing school assignments. This information distressed George as it was uncharacteristic of Mitch to rush any school projects. His day was methodically planned, a trait that Mitch had inherited from the store, as it was he who had stressed that the most satisfying results are achieved through careful preparation. Indeed, this training had contributed toward Mitch's excellent academic record and as a result, George Kovacs felt fortunate that he was able to enrich the young boy's life. Oh well, he thought, Mitch is a sensible boy. No sense getting alarmed over nothing.

Twinges of guilt gnawed at Mitch as he left the variety store. He regretted not being able to tell his friend of his plan which he hoped would increase the income of George Kovacs' store. However, he preferred that the old man only see the outcome of his efforts. With this in mind, Mitch headed north of Lundy Street, in the direction of the neighborhood library.

Once inside the library, Mitch headed straight to the subject index and flipped through the cards until he reached the section titled "Marketing." Scratching down some reference numbers, he then preceeded directly to the "stacks." Moving his forefinger along the backs of the books, Mitch finally found what he hoped would be a valuable contribution toward his plan — "101 Great Marketing Ideas." The remainder of the evening was devoted to reading the book. As well, Mitch made some brief notes and by the time his mother called "Lights out!" Mitch's marketing strategy was beginning to take shape.

The next day at school, Mitch went into the crowded lunchroom and headed for his usual table. Cathy, Sandra, and Tom were already seated and fortunately had taken the time to save him a chair.

"Hi gang!"

"Hi Mitch," they replied in unison.

"How'd you do on the Geography test, Mitch?" asked Cathy.

"88%. The test was pretty straightforward."

The three students nodded in agreement. Mitch took a sip of his milk and then toyed with the candy-striped straw.

"Hey people. I've got a big favor to ask."

In the next five minutes Mitch informed his friends of the plight of Kovacs' Variety Store and of his intended efforts to restore the store to the profitable times that it had once had.

"I think that's a really nice thing to do for that sweet old man. I'd be glad to lend a hand."

"Count me in," added Tom.

"Me three," added Sandra with a chuckle.

Mitch beamed with gratitude.

"I knew I could count on you guys. We'll meet after school in the library seminar room. See you there."

At three-thirty the four young people seated themselves at one of the long narrow library tables. Mitch began the meeting.

"Now I've got some ideas of my own, but since we're working as a group in this matter, I suggest that we 'brainstorm' like we do in Mr. Gibson's class and see what we come up with. Just keep in mind our key objective is to attract more customers to the variety store."

Within half an hour the group had hashed out a plan which was agreeable to all. From the library the group headed to the Art room where Sandra successfully persuaded Mr. Aiken, the Art teacher, into allowing the group the use of a variety of Art media. From these materials, posters were made which were to be displayed in the hallways of the school. These advertisements extolled the merits of the variety store and hopefully would entice the student body into spending their loose change at Kovacs' store.

Gazing at the brightly colored posters, Mitch began listing possible sites for them to be hung so that the students would constantly be aware of the marketing campaign. He also made a mental note to inform Mr. Willis, the school principal, of his intentions lest some over-zealous janitor tear down the posters. Silently he castigated himself for having overlooked such an important detail. Administrative permission would also be needed for the daily P. A. announcements that had been planned. These brief announcements would advertise a daily special that was being held at Kovacs' store. Mitch had read in "101 Great Marketing Ideas" that an excellent means of attracting customers was discount pricing. Furthermore, Mitch was sure that once inside the store, the students would purchase more than just the discount item.

Looking at the large office clock, Mitch saw that it was six o'clock, so he suggested to his friends that they head on home. Before doing so he thanked each of them for their efforts.

Throughout the following day Mitch and Tom kept an eye on the students' reaction towards their posters. During the lunch period Mitch and Cathy went to Mr. Willis with their plan. The principal was impressed with their genuine concern, so impressed in fact that he allowed the students the use of the office mimeograph machine so they could reproduce 1,000 copies of the "flyer" that Sandra had drawn up. This decorative handbill described Kovacs' Variety Store as an independent convenience store which had faithfully served the neighborhood for sixteen years.

After school, the four youths planned to distribute their flyers to those houses which were in the immediate vicinity of the store. Once again, this was an idea that had been stressed in the book that Mitch had read on marketing strategies. It had stated that a businessman must know his market and Mitch surmised that children and the neighborhood home owners were the most accessible market. Thanking Mr. Willis for his help, Mitch and Sandra said they'd come by after school for the completed handbills.

At five o'clock, Mitch rode his bike over to the Kovacs' Variety Store. He and his friends had finished delivering the handbills, so now it was time to inform his friend, the store owner, of the marketing whirlwind which was swirling about him. Leaning his bike against the plate glass store window, Mitch headed inside the store and was greeted by a smiling George Kovacs.

"Hey Mitch. Good to see you. You finish that school work?"

"Yeah. Sure George," Mitch replied, shouldering past a few young children who were mulling over the comic books.

"It's been a good day. There was a good sized group of students from your school in the store today."

Mitch smiled and leaned back against the large soda pop cooler. He then carefully outlined his plan to the older man. Kovacs sat silently on his stool. Shaking his head, he then gave forth a low whistle.

"What a businessman."

Mitch took out his note pad and together he and George Kovacs drew up a list of potential discount items.

"I'll have to do some extra ordering on these items," Kovacs said, gesturing at the list.

"Don't forget those family-size bottles of Coca Cola," replied Mitch over his shoulder.

The old man laughed and watched the boy head down the aisle of the store. He was still smiling as he reached for his order form.

Suggested Activities

1. What is invaluable in the neighborhood project outline? What would you change?
2. Design a marketing program for an item which you feel is needed at your school.
3. Role play a situation surrounding a theft at the store. How would Mitch deal with it?
4. Compare *The Old Man and the Sea* with this story.

Anson

> **Purpose:** **This story illustrates the plight of the gifted learner whose needs are not met within the regular classroom setting.**

"Ninety, ninety-one, ninety-two. That should do it."

"Not quite," said Mrs. Garrett. "We should have ninety-three students on board. Whom are we missing?"

The three grade 7 teachers looked at each other, patiently waiting for the responsible party to step forward.

Mrs. Whittington waited for the appropriate moment and then stepped forward.

"Well," she began, "Anson has maintained his no-show record for field trips."

The other two teachers smugly nodded their heads and waited for the usual explanation.

"He refuses to go. Says that there's no educational value in a trip to Canada's Wonderland. Moreover he maintains that such an outing is meant to be pleasurable so who are we to designate his company and restrict his whereabouts."

Mrs. Garrett shook her head.

"I failed him in History this year. He gave me the same illogical nonsense about projects."

"Oh well, one less body, one less worry," sighed Mrs. Whittington.

The teachers nodded agreement and then each climbed aboard their respective buses. With efficient, dutiful precision the engines of the school buses turned over and the drivers wheeled out into the moving traffic.

Anson Tierney stood by the portable, patiently watching the fleet move out. He toyed idly with the sheet of manilla paper that he held in his hand. Without looking at it, his prior experiences allowed him to recite the list by heart — Math — page 107, all parts; Spelling — Part C, any list; Grammar — copy and analyse the following sentences, and on and on. Instinctively, he crumpled the paper, marvelling at its compliancy and then drop-kicked the small bundle onto the asphalt. So what, he thought, I'll just say I misplaced it. Breaking into his best Frank Sinatra swagger he buoyantly began to hum the melody of "My Way" and proceeded into the school.

Looking down the hallway Anson realized that he'd reached what Frost referred to "as the fork in the road." If he went towards the left he would end up in the gym and that madman Harris would no doubt make him run laps or worse, try and engage him in a conversation about the metaphysical implications of squash. And yet, a step in the right direction and Anson would wind up in the jaws (or should that be bowels?) of the administration.

A voice broke in on his thoughts.

"Hey! Hey! Whatta ya doin' standin' where I'm tryin' to mop?"

"Huh? Oh . . . nothing, nothing at all."

"Well c'mon. I got work to do. Get to class. Isn't that where you're supposed to be?"

"They don't need me there," replied Anson, "so they've given up on me and let me wander the halls."

The janitor simply grunted. Anson watched the small man's thickly muscled arms effortless move the mop across the terazzo floor.

"Why bother?"

"What?" replied the janitor.

"Why bother?" repeated Anson. "By three-thirty the floor will be dirty again."

"It's my job. Besides I like to keep busy."

"Yes, but you're simply repeating the same process over and over. Do it once and save your energy for something more constructive."

"Such as?" asked the janitor.

"Search me," Anson mumbled. "Search me."

The old janitor looked at Anson, shook his head and silently went back to his mopping. The boy took this as a signal that the conversation had ended. Abruptly, Anson spotted a pair of red sweatpants advancing. Harris! Reluctantly, Anson moved in the direction of the office. Hoping to sneak by the dreaded place, he kept close to the wall. He envisioned the hot, white searchlight scanning the wall. He got up on his toes moving ever so softly. Just a few more steps and freedom. Freedom.

"Anson! Anson Tierney."

Trapped! Yes, he'd been trapped by the warden's secretary, Mrs. Hall.

"Yes, Mrs. Hall?"

"I was wondering if you could help me again with the Gestetner machine. The darn thing keeps cutting out on me and I've got to get eight hundred letters run off by 10:30 recess."

"Well, I'll see what I can do," he replied. Anything to keep the old girl from telling the warden he thought to himself.

He bent over the small green machine. Working deftly, he adjusted the vertical clamp and then raised the head of the fountain. The remaining feigned mechanics were pure "show biz." Might as well give ol' Mrs. Hall her money's worth he thought, smiling to himself. Finally, after the necessary pause, Anson straightened up and snapped on the machine. The old machine sputtered and then commenced to spit out P.T.A. invitations. Anson took a perfunctory bow and ambled out of the copying room with Mrs. Hall's profuse thanks echoing behind him.

Oh no! Those damn red sweatpants were advancing at an alarming pace. Quickly Anson bolted for the stairs, taking them two at a time. He paused on the top stair and basked in the narrowness of his escape. He considered how many times he had climbed these stairs. Sometimes three steps at a time, other times, in the presence of teachers, he'd taken them one at a time. Suddenly he smiled thinking about the time that Jenny Caruso, trying to race him up the stairs had fallen and then been reprimanded by Mrs. Prince, the stodgy grade 2 teacher.

He looked at his watch and realizing it was now 10 a.m., marvelled at how quickly the hour had passed. Oh well. Better check in at the library before Miss Parker sends out a search party.

Anson had always found solace in the library. As a class they spent forty-five minutes in this room each week and his homeroom teacher was wise enough to let them use the time for independent study purposes. The majority of his peers abused it and instead chose to carve their current flame's initials in the book shelves. However, Anson could always be found perched atop one of the large pillows, basking in the sunlight and totally absorbed in Wells, Bradbury, or possibly Wyndham. Anson often volunteered to stack chairs or file cards for Miss Parker. In return she gave him first crack at any new library materials.

He pushed the library door open. Good it was empty. Thank heavens for field trips he thought.

"Anson. Just the person I was looking for. Have you ever seen one of these before?"

He looked down at the strange cream-colored machine. It appeared as if someone had melted a typewriter with a portable television set.

"It's a microcomputer," said Miss Parker, who had judged his silent stare as a negative response. "How would you like to do me a favor and see if you can figure out how to operate the machine? You know how I am with instruction manuals."

Immediately Anson thought of a time last Christmas when Miss Parker had attempted to install a suspended film screen. Instead she had ripped out three ceiling tiles and fallen off the chair.

"Sure Miss Parker. I'll see what I can do. No promises and no bills if I break it."

Miss Parker laughed and walked away.

Anson plugged in the machine and found the "ON" switch. Pressing it, he heard that familiar sound, a sound that was musical to a video addict such as himself. The "READY" signal began its hypnotic flashing upon the screen. Flipping through the manual Anson settled on page nine and began to acquaint himself with the keyboard. His nimble fingers played upon the keys and produced his first message — ANSON TIERNEY ISS ON HOLI-DAY. Gazing at the screen he cursed his small error and then nodded his head in agreement with the message of the computer. Then with one deft flick he cleared the screen, again causing the computer to sing out and entice him further. By using the manual Anson was soon familiar with the keyboard. He vaguely heard the recess bell, but Miss Parker's sideways glance meant that he could ignore it.

"How are you making out Anson?" inquired the librarian.

"I'm not quite sure. What is a syntax error?"

"Well," she began, "let's just see."

Miss Parker pulled up a chair and explained a few minor details that Anson in his curious haste had glossed over. She then turned the pages of the manual to number 17, which dealt with small-scale programming.

"Go ahead. You can do it."

And so on it went. Every half-hour teacher and student would continue this pattern of consultation. Anson would reach a stumbling block and Miss Parker would patiently ease him over it. By the end of the school day Anson had completed a short printed program which dealt with a famous science fiction author. Carefully rolling the program, Anson then secured it with an elastic band.

"I think I'll show this to my Dad. He's quite an expert in the computer field."

Miss Parker nodded her head and returned to her card index.

Moving towards the door Anson suddenly paused.

"I thought you didn't know anything about computers, Miss Parker?"

She continued to shuffle the cards in the index file, yet before she could reply Anson was out the door and down the stairs. Turning past the office he saw the back of Mrs. Hall hunched over the whirling Gestetner machine. Anson simply smiled, waved his program in the direction of Mrs. Hall, and then headed out the door. He saw that the fleet of school buses had returned. The students filed off the buses clutching the day's bounty.

"Well Anson, you sure missed a great field trip. We went on the rides and saw all the best shows. How about you? How'd the day go?"

"Just great, Mike. Just great."

Suggested Activities

1. Role play a conversation between Anson and his guidance counsellor or principal.
2. Design a challenging program school day for Anson.
3. Write a vignette of Anson as principal twenty years later. What would his school be like?
4. What is the most frustrating aspect of giftedness? Draw a comic strip that illustrates your answer.

Withdrawn

Ann Geh
Teacher of the Gifted,
Dufferin County Board of Education

> **Purpose:** This story exemplifies many of the problems encountered by a gifted child who is withdrawn from regular classes to attend a special class for the gifted.

It was one of those wonderful April days when you know for certain that the worst of winter is over. Through the classroom window the sun's rays warmed and teased the children, making them restless to be outside. Even the janitor, unable to resist the beauty of the day, was busying himself in the mud puddled playground. Beyond the school grounds the trees had assumed that hazy brown blush created by the subtle swelling of hundreds of tiny buds. Birds were breaking the long silence of snow-softened winter with their excited calls and the unmistakable smell of warm damp earth drifted through the open window to mix with those of pencil sharpenings and bubble gum.

Melissa studied the line-up at Mrs. Potter's desk with resignation. There was no point in asking the teacher to read her story now, she would only have time for a perfunctory glance. It would be better to hand it in after school when it stood more chance of an uninterrupted reading. Melissa marvelled at Mrs. Potter's patience as she explained to Jamie for the third time that day that perimeter and area were different. There was never sufficient time to answer everybody's questions and although Melissa had never seen Mrs. Potter turn away an appeal for help, she knew that some children just grew tired of waiting and drifted away.

Melissa herself was a timid and undemanding child who sought a minimum of attention. For years she had dutifully conformed to the expectations of the class, achieving their antagonism. Instead she privately released her creative energies into an ever increasing stack of notebooks rapidly accumulating under her bed. In class she only answered questions directed specifically at her and only required the simplest instructions — if any — to complete her assignments. Increasingly there were times when she wished she weren't quite so competent and that her needs would justify a brief ten minutes of Mrs. Potter's time, in order to ask any one of the hundreds of questions that constantly bubbled to the surface of her mind, none of which appeared to be on the grade 4 curriculum.

All of her assigned work for the week was completed and as it was only Wednesday, she had two days to fill with activities of her own choosing. At the beginning of the year she had been so excited by this freedom to work independently, but recently she felt that she was working in a vacuum. Occasionally her best friend Jane joined her and then she had someone to discuss her research with, but today Jane was still plodding through her spelling exercises and Melissa was alone.

The library was deserted. Being a small country school their share of a librarian was a scanty 25 percent and today wasn't Mr. Jones' day. Melissa surveyed the familiar shelves of fiction in the hope that some new books may have come in, but she was unlucky. Since the school only went up to grade 5 there wasn't much beyond that level and she had long since exhausted the selection with her reading and re-reading. She turned her attention to the non-fiction and checked the card catalogue for "Rainbows", without success. Under "Weather" she located one book, but it proved to be a simple grade one book. In the encyclopedias her thirst for knowledge was rewarded with a few paragraphs about light rays, prisms, and refraction, but she thought sadly how it failed to capture the wonder and beauty she felt at the sight of a rainbow. She had almost finished writing those feelings when the bell interrupted her thoughts and she returned to the classroom. It was a flurry of bags, jackets, and boots. Mrs. Potter was surrounded by children vying for the last drops of her attention before catching their buses home.

Melissa placed her story on the pile to be marked, collected her lunch box and bag and joined up with Jane as they left the classroom. Her friend seemed very excited about something.

"You missed the good news," Jane said. "Mrs. Potter just announced that tomorrow Mr. Badgley is auditioning our class for the school play. It's going to be that one we had in our readers called 'The Canada Goose' — you remember."

Melissa did remember the play, it was humorous and patriotic, and she knew Jane would make an excellent lead.

"Oh, you would be a super Motto, Jane. Are you going to try out?"

"You bet," said Jane, "but I'll be competing with the grade 5s for the part, so it will be tough. What about you, which part would you like?"

"Oh you know I don't like acting, I get so embarrassed with all those people staring at me. I'm better at writing plays than acting in them."

They chattered excitedly about the forthcoming play as the school bus wound along the country roads, pausing at farm gates to disgorge small groups of children. Melissa arrived home first and waved to Jane as the bus pulled away. She turned and began the run between the avenue of trees towards the farmhouse at the same time that Bacchus, her exuberant Labrador, began his usual dash from the opposite direction. To a stranger a muddy collision appeared inevitable, but this had been a daily routine since Melissa's first day of Kindergarten and with great skill Bacchus slithered to a stop in front of Melissa for his customary hug. They ran side by side the rest of the way and Melissa opened the door with a cheery "Hi Mum."

"Hi, dear! I'm here, in the kitchen."

The house smelt of fresh paint noticed Melissa, obviously spring fever had affected her mother too. Mrs. Jenkins was putting potatoes in the oven and Neil was sitting on the floor surrounded by Lego. There were cookies and milk all ready on the table and they sat down as usual to exchange the day's news. Melissa noticed that her mother looked excited about something, as if she had some good news.

"You know those tests that you took at school last term, dear?"

Melissa nodded.

"Well we had a letter from the Board of Education today to tell us that you have been selected for enrichment classes next year."

Melissa smiled, feeling pleased and excited at the prospect. She knew from older children that they really enjoyed the classes. Her mother continued explaining the purpose of the classes. A question occurred to Melissa.

"Where will I have to go to the class, Mum?"

"The letter says it will be held at Elizabeth Street School, one day every two weeks."

"Oh. Mum, who else will be going from my class? Is Jane going?"

"I don't know dear, you'll have to ask her in the morning."

"Well, she's pretty smart. I'm sure she'll be going too."

"Just don't be too disappointed if she isn't," warned Mrs. Jenkins.

Melissa couldn't imagine school without Jane. They had been together since Kindergarten and she would hate to be separated.

The next morning when she sat down beside Jane in their usual seat on the bus, her first words were, "Did you get a letter about enrichment classes?"

"No," said Jane. "What are they anyway?"

"You know — those classes that Andrea and Peter go to from Grade 5."

It was apparent that Jane had not been notified and at first Melissa hoped that the letter might just have been delayed. As the days passed it became obvious that not only had Jane not been selected, but that no one else from their school had either. Melissa was to be the sole representative. Jane teased her quite a bit about it, calling her "Miss I.Q. 1983," and although Melissa tried to laugh it off she sensed that Jane was rather hurt and felt rejected. It made Melissa feel guilty about her own selection, as if she had betrayed Jane in some way. She made a point of avoiding the subject and as Jane was given the lead in the school play, the tension was eased and their friendship continued unscathed through the summer term.

School in September held few surprises for Melissa. She was familiar with both her classmates and her teacher from previous years. Her enrichment classes were not due to begin until the second week of term and her anticipation was only marred by the fact that she had no one with whom to share the experience. Occasionally she told her mother of her hopes and expectations, but it wasn't the same as discussing it with someone her own age. Jane appeared to have forgotten all about the classes, but Melissa knew as the first Tuesday neared that she would have to broach the subject. Monday night on the bus she mentioned as casually as she could, "See you on Wednesday. It's my first enrichment day tomorrow."

"Oh yeah. I'd forgotten about that. Well have a good time and tell me all you learn so that I can get smart too."

What a relief Melissa thought. Perhaps it was going to be all right after all. She would be able to share her experiences with Jane by telling her about it on the way home the next night.

Tuesday morning her mother had to drive her into school early to catch the bus to Elizabeth Street School. Melissa was surprised to see three other children waiting for the bus and recognized them as children who went out every day for special classes. They stared at her as she walked up and one of them spoke.

"Do you have to come to dumb class too?"

Melissa explained quietly that she was going to an enrichment class, hoping to silence them as quickly as possible, but her answer had the reverse effect. One of the children parrotted her reply and another laughingly asked,

"What do you know! Another new name for our class?" They all laughed raucously at each other's comments and Melissa attempted to find a seat away from them, but the bus was almost full and she had no alternative.

"I'm sitting with an enrichment kid. Think I'll get smart?" questioned her neighbor to the whole bus.

Melissa stared out of the window trying to ignore the sneering, giggling children and hoping the bus journey would pass quickly. She wondered if there were any other enrichment children on the bus, but didn't like to look around in case she attracted more attention. When she arrived at the office of the new school she discovered that there had in fact been four other enrichment children on the bus, but they had been in a group at the back. She was determined to sit with them on the way home.

The secretary directed them to a room along the hall. Although it was a regular classroom it seemed spacious to Melissa without the usual complement of thirty-five desks and chairs. They had been replaced by five large tables on which were a variety of books and equipment, including two computers and a model of the human brain. Melissa felt a surge of excitement. One third of the room was taken up by a circle of chairs in which some children were already sitting chatting with an adult, presumably the enrichment teacher. She introduced herself as Mrs. Woodham and after welcoming the children, asked them to introduce themselves. Melissa realized that she was the only single student from a school, the others were in groups of three or four. She would have to penetrate those natural groupings to form friendships. She was amazed to find that there were only to be twelve of them in the class. Each student was asked to talk about his or her interests or hobbies and Melissa was delighted to hear two other children express a desire to be writers. Beth had actually had something published in a national children's magazine. Published! The thought had never occurred to her beyond the realms of her own school newspaper.

One small boy called David said something which surprised her even more, he claimed that he found mathematics beautiful. To Melissa mathematics had always been a series of routine calculations to be performed as quickly as possible and the conviction in the boy's voice startled her.

Some children had new and unusual interests that fascinated her. Christine's family were ballooning enthusiasts and she suggested her father might be willing to bring in their balloon and inflate it in the school yard. Mrs. Woodham said she thought that was a wonderful idea and that she would discuss it with Christine's father. As the discussion continued and expanded to explore the purpose of the classes, Melissa felt the right little knot that she'd felt inside during the bus journey begin to dissolve and she surprised herself by contributing several times to the conversation.

Mrs. Woodham didn't seem to be worried that they should be getting on with some work and by the time she had outlined the focus of the program for the first time it was recess. Melissa, in an uncharacteristic burst of confidence, joined three girls from a neighboring school — Christine, Jennifer, and Beth. She was particularly attracted to Beth and felt she would like to know her better. The girls accepted her easily, but once outside they were spotted as strangers and drew some curious stares. One tall boy asked them who they were and what they were doing at "his school." Christine showed herself well able to cope with such badgering and told him firmly to "buzz off" if he couldn't be polite. Melissa knew it wouldn't have worked if she had said it, but something in Christine's voice cowed the boy and he left them alone.

After recess they began work in pairs on a variety of activities, including brain studies. Melissa worked with David and they enjoyed the experiments to test their most effective learning styles. Melissa had the opportunity to ask him why he thought math was so beautiful. He looked at her as if he didn't understand the question and then said slowly, "It's the patterns and the endless possibilities for finding out something new that I can make the numbers do."

Melissa was not sure she understood, but wondered if maybe she had missed something valuable in her math education.

The day passed more rapidly than any other school day she remembered — until the return journey. Because the other four enrichment children chose to sit together she was again forced to look for a seat with one of the other children. Someone stuck a foot out to trip her and then a boy shouted, "Come and sit with me — I need the contact with brains!"

"No, come here, I need it more!" someone else retorted. This began a game of students offering her a seat, but then sitting in it when she approached. The bus was in an uproar and Melissa was close to tears when she felt a quiet tug at her sleeve. It was one of the children from her class.

"Come and squeeze in with us."

Unfortunately the noise had gained the bus driver's attention and he came back and insisted that the rule was one person to a seat, and moved Melissa. The special education children cheered and Melissa blinked to keep back the tears. Why did this awful journey have to spoil such a good day?

She was relieved to spot Jane's familiar face when they finally arrived at her home school. She waved to catch her attention, but Jane seemed engrossed in conversation with Susan and didn't notice Melissa. Unwilling to risk the anger of other children by jumping to the front of the line-up and joining Jane, Melissa gave up and went to the back. When she got on the bus Jane and Susan were already sitting together and Melissa sank down in the first vacant seat, no longer caring who she was near, but just wanting to get home. She would have to tell Jane all about it in the morning.

Her mother looked at her expectantly as she entered the kitchen and was surprised at the subdued mood evident in Melissa's expression.

"Hi darling. How was your first class?"

"Oh fine, Mum, just fine thanks."

Mrs. Jenkins was used to Melissa's reticent nature and usually refrained from questioning her daughter when she obviously didn't want to talk, but something in Melissa's manner worried her.

"I've been wondering about you all day. I'm curious to know what you did. Come and tell me all about it."

"Oh the class was great Mum. I met some really neat kids who have all sorts of interesting hobbies and the work was about how we learn through our senses. My visual memory is my strongest sense."

Her enthusiasm returned as she told the day's happenings, but her face clouded as she remembered the bus journey.

"Mum, do I have to go on the bus? Couldn't you drive me to classes? Please?"

"I'm sorry dear, but you know Daddy needs the car on Tuesday mornings. I hardly had time to drive you to the local school this morning, let alone drive you right into town. What's the problem with the bus?"

"Oh, it's just this horrible bunch of kids who teased me and because I'm the only one from our school going I have to sit with them."

"Just ignore them dear, they'll soon get tired of teasing you."

"I tried Mum, I really did, but it didn't work. They just keep on and on saying the same stupid things and laughing."

Mrs. Jenkins knew that Melissa had never managed to form a protective shell against the cruelty of other children. She just seemed to absorb the hurt, unable to defend herself. It was the same hyper-sensitivity that enabled her to respond so acutely to the world around her and to write her poetry. Gently her mother asked Melissa to imagine what the other special education children — the non-enrichment ones — might have suffered when they had been "identified."

"They probably see you as a perfect target for revenge, which doesn't justify their behavior, but it may help you to understand it."

Melissa did remember how cruel some children had been to a Down's Syndrome child in her class once. He had never been really accepted and was always fair game when the teachers weren't around to protect him. A horrible thought struck her.

"Mum, am I going to be seen as some kind of freak from now on?"

"I don't think so dear. You always got on well with your class and Jane has always been a loyal friend. It shouldn't make any difference."

The image of Jane giggling and talking with Susan flashed into Melissa's mind and her mother's words held little reassurance.

Her fears were justified the next morning on the bus. Jane was sitting in a window seat with Susan by her side and pretended not to see Melissa. Melissa's heart sank. She had to talk this thing out with Jane. It was recess before she had the chance and even then she had to catch hold of Jane's coat to get her attention.

"Jane, can we talk please?"

"Oh my goodness, look who's giving me an audience!" Jane announced to anyone within earshot.

"Don't be like that Jane," begged Melissa. "I haven't had a chance to talk to you since Monday."

"Too good for me now that you go to enrichment classes, eh? I supposed you met some better friends there."

"Jane, that's not true. I did meet some nice kids but that doesn't mean I don't still want to be friends with you."

"Then why didn't you sit with me on the bus last night?" retorted Jane.

"I saw you with Susan and I'd had such a miserable time on the bus from town that I just wanted to be alone," Melissa explained.

"Well if you want to be alone, that's just fine with me. Come on Susan, race you to the climber."

Melissa was left standing alone at the edge of the playground, wondering why her once secure, familiar world seemed to be so distorted. Obviously Jane's jealousy and hurt were deeper than she had thought.

After recess she sat miserably at her desk wondering if her friendship with Jane could be salvaged. She was unaware of the math drill in progress, until she felt everyone looking at her expectantly. There was an uncomfortable silence as she searched the boards for some clue as to what was going on. A loud stage whisper was heard.

"She doesn't know. I thought she was supposed to know everything."

The ensuing giggles were silenced by Mrs. Potter, who repeated the question for Melissa's benefit.

"Twelve times eleven, Melissa."

She answered quickly and in her haste said one hundred and twenty-one instead of one hundred and thirty-two. She corrected herself immediately, but there were more giggles and comments as Melissa reddened.

Was everyone against her? Wasn't she even allowed to make one mistake now? One wrong answer and they were ready to pounce on her. She thought she knew them all so well and yet they seemed like strangers now. She wanted to stand up and shout, "Hey! It's me — Melissa Jenkins. I was in Kindergarten with you, remember? What has changed? What have I done wrong?"

Returning home that evening she hugged Bacchus for a longer time than usual, taking comfort from his unwavering loyalty. Sometimes, she thought, I feel closer to Bacchus than any human. By the time she went to bed she had made up her mind. She would drop out of enrichment. As much as she enjoyed it, she couldn't live for that one day of acceptance out of two weeks of rejection. She had never felt so isolated and lonely before. Tearfully she told her mother of her decision.

"I don't feel I belong in my regular class anymore. Everybody seems out to get me just because I go to enrichment. Well I'll stop going out and then everything will be normal again."

Her mother was sympathetic and talked with her for a long time. She succeeded in calming Melissa and persuading her to give the class one more try, and also to let things settle down with the other children.

"Give them time dear, they have to adjust to the new situation too. Gradually they will see that you haven't really changed."

Melissa wasn't sure how long she could wait, but hoped fervently that her mother was right.

It was an uncomfortable two weeks. Little tricks were played on her; one day the laces from her running shoes disappeared and another day she found a notice on her desk saying, "Reserved for Miss I.Q." She knew who that was from. Gradually the jibes did subside, but Melissa felt she always had to be on her guard in case anything she said or did gave them an excuse to ridicule her. Jane continued to avoid her and carried on an ostentatious friendship with Susan and her group, involving great note passing and giggling.

Melissa woke on the second enrichment day with a sick feeling of apprehension about the bus ride. It was hard to look forward to the day when she felt as if she had to run a gauntlet first. Her mother offered to wait for the bus with her, an offer she gladly accepted, but later regretted. Once on the bus the taunts came thick and fast.

"Mummy came with her today to protect her."

"So smart she can't wait for the bus by herself."

"Leave me alone," whispered Melissa as firmly as she could muster.

"Stop it! Leave me alone!" they mimicked. Even in her unhappiness it struck her as incongruous that she should be asking to be left alone when she felt so desperately lonely. If only one more child came to the class from her school, she felt the situation might have been tolerable.

At the Elizabeth Street School she walked dejectedly into the classroom. She heard a voice say, "Hi, Melissa! How are things with you?"

Looking up she saw Beth and Christine smiling at her. She had almost forgotten about them in the intervening weeks, it was good to see friendly faces again.

The children were already involved in a lively discussion and Melissa was surprised to discover that it focused on problems they had encountered in their regular classes because of enrichment. Some children missed music or sports practice and some complained about having to get up earlier. One girl had returned to find several things missing from her desk. Several of them were disgruntled at having to catch up with missed work. Christine laughingly said that her only problem was that the classes were too infrequent and several agreed with her, though Melissa shrank at the thought of more bus journeys. Somehow, thought Melissa, their problems didn't sound as devastating as hers. Even David, who had been beaten up in the school yard, spoke as if he almost expected it. Melissa had been silent up to this part and Mrs. Woodham asked her if she had anything to contribute.

She began hesitantly, telling them about the teasing on the bus and the ostracism in class. Somehow it sounded silly and unimportant, especially compared to David's experiences, but no one laughed. When she looked up she saw several students nodding agreement. She found they had all had similar experiences to a greater or lesser degree. Mrs. Woodham suggested that they brainstorm ways of coping with the adverse reactions of their regular classmates and Melissa listened carefully, hoping to find an answer. She was disappointed. She had tried those suggestions unsuccessfully.

Ignoring the problem had not made it disappear and she certainly wasn't the type to try physical force. Neither did she feel that her own behavior had been arrogant enough to have merited the treatment she received. There was no magic solution after all. From now on she would have to expect the teasing and taunting — if she decided to continue attending the class.

At recess Mrs. Woodham came over to Melissa.

"It's been really difficult for you socially, hasn't it Melissa?" she began. Melissa nodded, saying nothing.

"It will improve you know. The children will eventually realize that you are basically the same person as before."

Just what her mother had said thought Melissa. It was easy to give advice when you didn't have to live with the problem all week. She had heard enough advice, she was the one suffering, she would have to find her own answer.

That afternoon Mrs. Woodham recommended a whole list of books to them. Several of the authors — C. S. Lewis, Tolkien, Madeleine L'Engle — were familiar to Melissa. Mrs. Woodham wanted each of them to choose a book to take home, read, and report on the following session. Melissa chose a book she had never seen before, cheered by the prospect of some new reading material. The book was called *Keeper of the Isis Light* by Monica Hughes. She began to read it on the way home and as was her habit, became so immersed that she was oblivious to the calls of "book-worm" from her tormentors. Getting no flicker of response from her, they soon turned their attention to other distractions. It was true then, ignoring them did work — if it was complete enough. She did have the power to protect her vulnerability by absorbing herself in something else.

By the time she put out her light later that night she had finished the whole book. She lay awake in the darkness thinking about Olwen, the main character, a young girl raised in isolation by a robot on the imaginary planet Isis. It was easy to identify with Olwen, both she and Melissa were segregated because of their deviation from the norm. Olwen was perceived as deformed, in spite of the fact that her physical differences better adapted her to life on Isis, whereas Melissa was rejected because of mental superiority. Being different, even in a superior way, was a passport to loneliness, thought Melissa, except perhaps in sports. The good athletes were always popular and she wondered why it didn't apply to brains too.

Just as Olwen had been happy before the arrival of the colonists who pointed out her differences, Melissa had been accepted and happy prior to her "identification." How she hated that word! Her problem, she now saw, was not of her own making anymore than Olwen's was. The problem lay in other people's attitudes, perceptions, and fears. The question was, could she hide her mental ability any more effectively than Olwen could hide her scaly green skin or enlarged nostrils? How much longer was she willing to hold back, to conform, in order to gain peer approval?

Olwen had refused to compromise and had chosen instead a lonely life. Melissa wondered if she were strong enough to do that. She remembered Christine's confidence and David's lack of concern in the face of physical danger. She fell asleep and dreamed that she was striding fearlessly across Isis with Olwen by her side.

Suggested Activities

1. Using the theme of alienation/isolation, take the control character from a book that explicates this particular theme, and compose a profile, focusing upon reasons/effects of isolation/alienation. Suggest remediation techniques.

2. Retell the story from a point of view other than that of Melissa (that is, a classmate in her enrichment program).

3. Research the life of a person in history who has been persecuted for his/her beliefs/values, beliefs which time proved to be correct. Present your product in a non-conventional manner (for example, tape, slides, play, poetry).

Music and the Savage Beast

> **Purpose:** A gifted musician conceals his talent until circumstances force him to reveal his true ability. Once again we note the problems of being gifted/talented in a world that doesn't always appreciate such gifts.

Blair Tindall sat down wearily and waited for it to begin. Just as an experienced sailor learns to compare the savagery of each storm with previous ones, so too had Blair taken to measuring his classmates' tirades against him. At times they were preoccupied with more pressing matters, such as a class test, and Blair was allowed a brief respite from their taunts. However, when school boredom peaked, as it seemed to frequently, the baiting by the class bullies became relentless. Suddenly a boy jumped out of his seat, squared his shoulders, tucked his books in the crook of his arm and began to strut down the aisle.

"Who am I?" he screamed with malicious exuberance.

"Wally."

"Gimp."

"Loser," replied the faceless chorus in unison.

Blair Tindall gripped the edges of his desk feeling a tremor run through his body. Laughter cut through the room and the anxious boy's uneasiness grew. Staring directly ahead he tried to focus on the classroom clock. To Blair's dismay, the front of the room began to perform a murky dance, as if his eyes had been daubed with vaseline.

"Okay, that's quite enough!", said a voice coming from the direction of the doorway. "Take out your books and let's get some work done."

The class clown clapped Blair on the back while at the same time he flashed a triumphant grin towards the class.

"Hurry up Doug. Take your seat!", commanded the teacher in an irritated voice.

Taking a deep breath, Blair eased his grip on the desk and then opened his notebook. The woman at the front of the room, a first-year teacher, glanced his way, but quietly moved in an opposite direction indicating the hopelessness of the situation. In Blair's mind, the classroom abuse was becoming unbearable. Why were they doing this to him? What had he done that was so terrible? The questions swirled about in his mind, yet did little to ease his present state of anguish. He'd undergone a similar problem at his old school last year, and now like some unexplained chinook, the past was recurring.

Relishing the silence that had fallen upon the room, he let his mind drift, and soon found himself thinking about St. Raymond's, his former school. It was there that Bob Gauthier, an older, foul-mouthed student, had begun teasing Blair about the fact that he and his younger sister, Louise, walked home together. Instantly Blair had felt the blood rise to his face and he'd sworn at Gauthier. His bravery had earned him a bloodied nose. From then on Gauthier and company, for lack of anything better to do, had tormented him constantly. Eventually, what had started as a diversionary game became a way of life. After two months of misery Blair had cracked. He stayed at home in bed for two days and left his sister to walk to school by herself.

Upon learning about the problem at school, his parents had confronted the school principal and naturally enough Gauthier had been punished. From this point on Blair had been a marked man at St. Raymond's. The students continued to confront him. The difference was that they learned to do it with subtlety.

At the end of the school year his father accepted a transfer to the east end of town and the children were enrolled in St. Benedict, a school that was much smaller than the previous one.

During the summer his father had given him a book to read entitled *The Martin Luther King Story*. He spoke to Blair about the importance of standing up for one's beliefs. Blair was confused. What did he have to stand up for? Or, more simply, how do you confront a faceless enemy, particularly if you have offended no one? However, Blair was able to cull from his father's words the fact that you should never lose your temper in front of your schoolmates. This reaction was viewed as a sign of weakness, and an area to be probed and prodded. Thus, for Blair Tindall, reaction meant no action.

Recognizing his stoic stance, the class' number one bully, Doug Johnson, who, as fate would have it, was a cousin of Bob Gauthier, developed a very straightforward strategy. During confrontations he was as loud as possible and always attacked in a place from which Tindall had no escape. This afforded the bully a captive audience. Classrooms, where the teacher exercised minimal authority, and recess periods were considered the best times for going after Blair.

Since the whole point of this cruel exercise was reaction, Blair had turned out to be a very disappointing victim. Recently, class scorn had been directed towards the bullies rather than Blair. Sensing defeat, the bullies had given up on verbal abuse and were now resorting to physical roughhousing. This action was too much for even Blair Tindall's case-hardened resolve.

The voice of the teacher interrupted his thoughts and slowly he became aware of tomorrow's homework assignment. Before the recess bell rang, Doug Johnson, on his way to the pencil sharpener, dropped a note on Blair's desk. Unfolding it, he read the tersely worded statement, "Recess time — you're done!" He slipped the note inside his notebook and tensely began to eye the clock. His sick anxiety proved to be ill-founded. The threatened violence never erupted as the teacher asked Blair to do some laminating at recess. Looking skyward he thanked God for having answered his prayers. However, this brief respite only served to whet the appetite of the bullies. It was not surprising then to anyone present in the boys' change room that afternoon to see four of the more boisterous class members surrounding Blair.

"Wally's gonna get it," someone whispered.

"Hey Blair buddy," said Doug, as a wicked grin crossed his face, "you missed your appointment this morning."

Whomp! The sound of Johnson's fist connecting with Blair's ribs made the other boys wince. Blair doubled over in pain prompting the other three boys to get their licks also. All of them aimed at his body, since facial punches left marks and that led to trouble with the office. Silently the remaining boys went about the business of getting changed while the bullies congratulated themselves on their bravery. Many of the students were angry with themselves for acting so cowardly in the face of such brutality and yet they were also thankful that the bullies had not singled them out for such treatment. With mixed emotions they filed past Blair, who was huddled in the corner of the room, and headed out into the gymnasium. As the bullies passed Blair they laughed.

"There's lots more where that came from," cried Johnson.

With a sigh Blair rubbed at his face with the sleeve of his sweatshirt. He considered reporting the incident, but then decided against this action since it would only result in another beating. Wearily he lifted himself off the floor and sat down wondering how much more he could endure.

"Hey Wally."

Blair glanced up. It was Doug Johnson.

"Teacher sent me to tell you to get your tail out there. So c'mon, let's move!", he said, almost spitting the words at Blair. "Oh, and one other thing. You keep your mouth shut about our little chat, okay?"

Blair nodded and followed Johnson out the door.

"What kept you?", inquired the teacher.

Suddenly he noticed that the eyes of the class were upon him. Clearing his throat he spoke.

"I broke a shoelace so I had to retie my shoe. Sorry, Miss Fisher."

She nodded and shifted her gaze from Blair to the entire class. "Now in case anyone hasn't heard, the school is having its annual talent show this month and as always there'll be a gymnastics routine performed. Do I have any volunteers?"

A smattering of hands were thrust in the air and the teacher smiled.

"Good. Practice begins tonight at 3:30. Okay, let's spread out and do some stretching."

Within seconds the class became a mass of twisting bodies. Forty-five minutes later, the gymn class ended.

"Blair would you help wheel these basketballs into the storage room?"

"Sure, Miss Fisher."

Pushing the cart across the gym he thought about the teacher's earlier announcement. He'd never been at a school that had a talent show.

"Excuse me, Miss Fisher, but what kind of talent is the school looking for?"

"Huh? . . . Oh, you mean the show. Well any kind I imagine. Dramatic, comical, musical. I'm sure the gymnastics display will fit into all three of those categories. Are you interested in the gymnastics routine?"

"No, music is my interest."

"That's Mr. Rasmussen's area," she replied, locking the storage room, "so maybe you should go and see him."

"Thanks, I will."

This new interest temporarily took Blair's mind away from the bullies at a time when such an escape was desperately needed. But then again, his guitar had always had a magical effect upon his life. Blair had played the guitar for the past four years and according to his instructors, he was "a natural." He appreciated the accolades, but more importantly he treasured the release that music provided. Recognizing their son's love of music, his parents had recently bought him a four-track tape recorder, a gizmo which enabled Blair to record over the same piece of tape four times and in a sense, create a one-man band. With the help of his guitar teacher, who was a member of a local rock band, he'd learned the intricacies of both the machine and the guitar. As Blair made his way down the hallway he decided that he'd see Mr. Rasmussen after school and show these kids at St. Benedict that he was more than just a punching bag.

After school that same day, Blair approached Mr. Rasmussen with guarded optimism. The little man was St. Benedict's only music teacher and for the past year Blair had been under Rasmussen's direction as a member of the school band. Yet Blair saw this as being no great advantage as he was a member of the woodwind section. Mr. Rasmussen had failed to gain a place with the city's largest orchestra and now held a life-long grudge against the melodious woodwind instrument.

Carefully, Blair pushed open the music room door. The teacher was reclining in a chair behind his desk, fiddling with the keys of a trumpet and cradling the brass instrument as if it were a tender infant.

"Excuse me, sir."

The little man slowly raised his head. "Tindall. What can I do for you?"

"Well, sir, I was wondering if I could audition for the talent show?"

"Playing a flute?", sputtered the teacher.

"No sir," replied Blair, somewhat irritated, "playing the guitar."

"You know how to play?", asked Mr. Rasmussen, as he resumed his toying with the trumpet.

"What a jerk," thought Blair. He would have loved to say that no sir he didn't know how to play and only wanted to go up on stage and bang the guitar like some village idiot. But, of course, he didn't.

"Yes sir, I've played the guitar for four years."

The music teacher pretended not to hear and instead raised the trumpet to his lips and blew into it. Blair pursed his lips, trying hard not to laugh at the discordant sounds Rasmussen was producing. Finally the teacher spoke.

"After school tomorrow. And be on time. There are five other kids trying out and I don't want to be here all night."

"Thank you, sir."

With that, Blair made a swift retreat from the room for fear that the teacher would again do his one-lipped imitation of Chuck Mangione.

Later that evening after both dinner and homework had been completed, Blair headed to the basement and began to practice for the audition. He began by switching on the tape machine and simply playing a wide variety of pieces. During the playback he listened intently, noting both the good and bad points of each song and chose the three songs with which he felt most comfortable.

The first was a slow-paced jazz song that dated back to the late fifties.

Blair's second choice, "Pinball Wizard," was much more contemporary. While playing this number Blair used an acoustic guitar which he knew would disappoint the rockers in the school, but having recently heard a radio interview with the song's composer, Pete Townsend, he'd sensed that the legendary guitarist had intended this song to convey a classical sound. Blair's final number was an original composition in which he displayed his deft fingerwork and solid picking. After endless repetitions of these three songs, Blair's fingers began to stiffen so he packed his equipment away and headed to bed both nervous and excited.

The next day at school was similar to many of the days that Blair had already experienced at St. Benedict's. Long, drawn out classes, mundane homework, and unfortunately, the continued taunts of the bullies. During French class Doug Johnson, who sat behind him, had blown spitballs into his hair, much to the delight of the class. The teacher, Monsieur Valleau, had again chosen to ignore his antics, which only added to Blair's distress.

As Blair sat there, red-faced and disgraced, he began to realize that in some ways he resembled many of the legendary recording artists whom he idolized. Once again he recalled the Pete Townsend radio interview in which the guitarist had described himself as having experienced some lonely adolescent years due to his oversized nose. At this point in his life Townsend resolved to become famous and to ensure that his face, nose and all, would be plastered over every magazine and newspaper in England. "Maybe I won't become famous," thought Blair, "but at least I'll prove to them that I'm more than just a Wally." With even greater resolve he continued his vigil over the classroom clock.

Finally the three-thirty bell rang. Racing to his locker, Blair quickly dumped his books on the top shelf and then headed straight to the music room. In his great haste, Blair mistakenly bumped into Doug Johnson.

"Hey Wally, what's the rush? Have to get home to water the flowers?" Johnson's cronies bellowed with laughter.

"Sorry Doug," said Blair, slowly backing away from the larger boy.

Johnson eyed him curiously but said nothing. Blair, seeing an escape opportunity, darted off down the hall. However, if he'd taken the time to turn around he'd have noticed that he was being followed.

Sure enough, Blair had no sooner arrived in the music room, than in walked Johnson and his head goon, Todd Beckley.

"Tindall you're late," said the easily irritated Mr. Rasmussen. "What do you want?", he added, looking in the direction of the two unexpected arrivals.

The two boys were momentarily speechless as Blair set up his equipment.

"Uh . . . we're here to see Wally, the rock star."

Rasmussen shook his head and sat down. One more powerless school teacher thought Blair.

"Well let's go Tindall. Get on with it."

Blair exhaled deeply, positioned his Gretsch guitar and gave it a few tenuous strums. He heard the boys snicker, while Rasmussen stifled a yawn. Recognizing his cue, Blair hit the opening chords to "Summertime," a haunting, melodious song that was played mostly on the upper neck of his guitar. Midway through the piece Blair glanced up and saw Rasmussen leaning forward in his chair. At the end of the number, with the last note still echoing throughout the room, the music teacher broke into applause. Blair dismissed his enthusiasm and exchanged the electric guitar for the acoustic instrument. With great intensity he fingered the opening notes to ''Pinball Wizard'' and then began some furious strumming. Halfway through the song, electric with courage, Blair glanced towards the back of the room. Beckley and Johnson were mouthing the words to the song, immersed in the sounds that he was creating. For the first time in a long while Blair allow-ed himself a small smile and then returned to the business at hand.

Suggested Activities

1. Write about a Blair Tindall that you have known.
2. Define escapism. Why is it sometimes needed? How do you escape?